EVALUATING TRAINING EFFECTIVENESS

Latest Titles in the McGraw-Hill Training Series

SELF-DEVELOPMENT
A Facilitator's Guide
David Megginson
and Mike Pedler   ISBN 0-07-707460-2

DEVELOPING WOMEN THROUGH TRAINING
A Practical Handbook
Liz Willis and
Jenny Daisley   ISBN 0-07-707566-8

DESIGNING AND ACHIEVING COMPETENCY
A Competency Based Approach to Developing People and
Organizations
Rosemary Boam and
Paul Sparrow   ISBN 0-07-707572-2

CAREER DEVELOPMENT AND PLANNING
A Guide for Managers, Trainers and Personnel Staff
Malcolm Peel   ISBN 0-07-707554-4

SALES TRAINING
A Guide to Developing Effective Sales People
Frank Salisbury   ISBN 0-07-707458-0

TOTAL QUALITY TRAINING
The Quality Culture and Quality Trainer
Brian Thomas   ISBN 0-07-707472-6

CLIENT-CENTRED CONSULTING
A Practical Guide for Internal Advisers and Trainers
Peter Cockman, Bill Evans and
Peter Reynolds   ISBN 0-07-707685-0

Details of these and other titles in the series are available from:

The Product Manager, Professional Books, McGraw-Hill Book Company Europe,
Shoppenhangers Road, Maidenhead, Berkshire, SL6 2QL.
Telephone: 0628 23432 Fax: 0628 770224

Evaluating training effectiveness

Translating theory into practice

Peter Bramley

McGRAW-HILL BOOK COMPANY

London · New York · St Louis · San Francisco · Auckland
Bogotá · Caracas · Hamburg · Lisbon · Madrid · Mexico · Milan
Montreal · New Delhi · Panama · Paris · San Juan · São Paulo
Singapore · Sydney · Tokyo · Toronto

Published by
McGRAW-HILL Book Company Europe
Shoppenhangers Road, Maidenhead, Berkshire SL6 2QL, England.
Telephone 0628 23432
Fax 0628 770224

British Library Cataloguing in Publication Data
Bramley, Peter
  Evaluating training effectiveness.
  1. Personnel, Training, Effectiveness, Assessment.
I. Title
658.312404

ISBN 0-07-707331-2

Library of Congress Cataloging-in-Publication Data
Bramley, Peter
  Evaluating training effectiveness: translating theory into
  practice/Peter Bramley.
      p.   cm. — (The McGraw-Hill training series)
    Includes bibliographical references and index.
    ISBN 0-07-707331-2
    1. Employees—Training of—Evaluation. I Title. II. Series.
HF5549.5.T7B63   1990
658.3'12404—dc20   90—41404

345 BP 9432

Typeset by Book Ens Limited, Baldock, Herts
Printed and bound in Great Britain by The Bath Press, Avon

Contents

Series preface

Training and development are now firmly centre stage in most organizations, if not all. Nothing unusual in that—for some organizations. They have always seen training and development as part of the heart of their businesses. More and more must see it the same way.

The pressure is on for them to do so. This pressure is coming from varied sources. The government, the CBI, the unions, the BIM, the new TECs, the EC and foreign competition are all exerting pressure—not just for more training, but for more relevant, appropriate and useful training.

In addition, the demographic trends through the nineties will inject into the market place severe competition for good people who will need good training. Young people without conventional qualifications, skilled workers in redundant crafts, people out of work, women wishing to return to work—all will require excellent training to fit them to meet the job demands of the 1990s and beyond.

But excellent training does not spring from what we have done well in the past. T&D specialists are in a new ball game. 'Maintenance' training—training to keep up skill levels to do what we have always done—will be less in demand. Rather, organization, work and market change training are now much more important and will remain so for some time. Changing organizations and people is no easy task, requiring special skills and expertise which, sadly, many T&D specialists do not possess.

To work as a 'change' specialist requires us to get to centre stage—to the heart of the company's business. This means we have to ask about future goals and strategies and even be involved in their development, at least as far as T&D polices are concerned.

This demands excellent communication skills, political expertise, negotiating ability, diagnostic skills—indeed, all the skills a good internal consultant requires.

The implications for T&D specialists are considerable. It is not enough merely to be skilled in the basics of training, we must also begin to act like business people and to think in business terms and talk the language of business. We must be able to resource training not just from within but by using the vast array of external resources. We must be able to manage our activities as well as any other manager. We must share in the creation and communication of the company's vision. We must never let the goals of the company out of our sight.

In short, we may have to grow and change with the business. It will be hard. We shall not only have to demonstrate relevance but also value for money and achievement of results. We shall be our own boss, as accountable for results as any other line manager, and we shall have to deal with fewer internal resources.

The challenge is on, as many T&D specialists have demonstrated to me over the past few years. We need to be capable of meeting that challenge. This is why McGraw-Hill Book Company (UK) Limited have planned and launched this major new training series—to help us meet that challenge.

The series covers all aspects of T&D and provides the knowledge base from which we can develop plans to meet the challenge. They are practical books for the professional person. They are a starting point for planning our journey into the twenty-first century.

Use them well. Don't just read them. Highlight key ideas, thoughts, action pointers or whatever, and have a go at doing something with them. Through experimentation we evolve; through stagnation we die.

I know that all the authors in the McGraw-Hill Training Series would want me to wish you good luck. Have a great journey into the twenty-first century.

ROGER BENNETT
Series Editor

About the series editor

Roger Bennett has over 20 years experience in training, management education, research and consulting. He has long been involved with trainer training. He has carried out research into trainer effectiveness and conducted workshops, seminars and conferences on the subject around the world. He has written extensively on the subject including the book *Improving Trainer Effectiveness*, Gower. His work has taken him all over the world and has involved directors of companies as well as managers and trainers.

Roger Bennett has worked in engineering, several business schools (including the International Management Centre, where he launched the UK's first masters degree in T&D) and has been a board director of two companies. He is the editor of the *Journal of European Industrial Training* and was series editor of the ITD's *Get In There* workbook and video package for the managers of training departments. He now runs his own business called The Management Development Consultancy.

Acknowledgement

I would like to express my thanks to Ruth Nissim for her encouragement and help during the preparation of this book. It was written during a particularly busy period at work and there were times when I considered whether to abandon the project. Without her encouragement I might have done so. Ruth also read all the drafts, discussed some of the issues and offered many very helpful suggestions. Her help has made it a much better book than the one I originally wrote.

Introduction

Why does someone write a book like this? It is very flattering to be asked to do it, but after some consideration of how much work is involved, flattery is not enough. It is certainly not for the money! In my case it is possible to trace it back to a specific event. The ultimate accolade for an American academic who is interested in training is to be asked to review the literature in the *Annual Review of Psychology*. Training in organizations is reviewed every four or five years. In the 1980 review, Goldstein deplored the lack of research published in training journals. In the 1984 review, Wexley deplored the lack of research published in training journals and dismissed most of the articles as being of the 'I tried it this way and it worked' type. In the 1988 review, Latham discussed only those articles which had been published in academic journals and did not bother to read training journals. His view was that, 'What remains elusive is the ability of training research to bring about relatively permanent changes in the behaviour of the practitioner' (1988, p546). When I read that, I felt that I wanted to take up the challenge. Of course it is possible to bridge this gap between practitioners and those who are carrying out research, but it will not happen naturally or automatically. It is an objective in and of itself. I thought that I would be able to use material which I had been developing with trainers in workshops, and expand it to form a more substantial contribution to this necessary, but neglected, area of linking research and theory with practice.

Training efficiency and effectiveness

When organizations ask for my help in evaluating their training activities, they invariably want to know whether the training was efficient, i.e. 'Has the programme achieved most of its objectives in a reasonably economic way?' This question can be quite simply answered by assessing the changes achieved during training and perhaps by examining the process.

If an organization were to pose the more difficult question of 'Was the training effective?', this would involve a more complex analysis. It would imply not only finding out whether the training was well done but also asking whether it was worth while for the organization to be sponsoring.

Definitions of training

Now one might expect the value of training to be assessed like that of other organizational functions; that is by its contribution to organizational goals. The fact that organizations are asking the first type of question (about efficiency) rather than the second type (about effectiveness) is a consequence of their definition of training which assumes that it is a process of adding to the skills of an individual. Using such a definition makes it difficult for them to formulate questions about changes in organizational effectiveness or contributions to organizational goals when thinking about the evaluation of training.

The process of training employees within an organizational context is defined in different ways by different authors. Two typical ones are given here to emphasize that clarity of definition is necessary because this controls the questions which can legitimately be raised.

A typical British definition is offered by the Department of Employment Glossary of Training Terms (1971): 'The systematic development of the attitude/knowledge/skill/behaviour pattern required by an individual to perform adequately a given task or job'.

The key concepts here are:

- 'Systematic development', which implies planning and control
- 'Individual', which excludes group and team development
- Job or task performance which is the criterion of success

One can see a strong link between this definition and the long tradition of industrial, technical training which is part of our culture. The definition has strengths in that it emphasizes a systematic process for improving work-based performance. Its weakness lies in the exclusion of groups and teams, thereby it ignores important aspects of the organizational context.

A typical American definition is very different, for example the one offered by Hinrichs (1976) is: 'Any organizationally initiated procedures which are intended to foster learning among organizational members in a direction contributing to organizational effectiveness.'

The key concepts are:

- 'Organizational procedures', which put the process into an organizational context
- 'Foster learning', which implies that the responsibility is shared between the organization offering it and the members receiving it
- The criterion of success is 'organizational effectiveness'

The USA has a long tradition of integrating people of widely different cultures into the nation. This has influenced the Organizational Development movement with its strong emphasis on making people feel that they belong. It also influences the definitions which are used for training and development activities. The definition offered by Hinrichs is much broader than the previous one and it would allow the inclusion of many organizational development activities as well as technical training. The strength of the definition is that it firmly plants training in its organizational context.

The synthesis of the necessary core concepts which I draw from these definitions and others like them, can be summarized in the following statements:

1 Training should be a systematic process with some planning and control rather than random learning from experience
2 It should be concerned with changing concepts, skills and attitudes of people treated both as individuals and as groups
3 It is intended to improve performance in both the present and the following job and through this should enhance the effectiveness of the part of the organization in which the individual or group works

Implications for evaluation

These concepts underpin some of the definitions which will be used in this book. It will be argued that education can be defined by the first two of these statements and thus the evaluation of education could be satisfied by some assessment of the systematic process and the changes. The examination of the process and the changes attributable to training is necessary, and will answer questions about *efficiency*. The third statement will be used to distinguish training from education in organizations. This implies that training in organizations must include an assessment of improvements in individual and organizational performance. This means asking questions about *effectiveness*.

The title of this book is *Evaluating Training Effectiveness* and this is a deliberate choice of words. It is not possible to divorce training in organizations from the concept of effectiveness. Nor can the concept of evaluation be separated from the training process.

The format of the book is shaped by the definition of training which I have adopted. The first part addresses the process of training; the second considers methods of measuring changes at individual, group and organizational levels. These two parts of the book will be of most value for trainers and training managers who are looking for practical advice. The third part of the book deals with the broader issues of various purposes for evaluation and strategies to meet these. This higher level of abstraction is necessary in order to consider the more political aspects of evaluating within an organizational context and this part will be of most use to training and personnel managers. Line managers also have some responsibility for evaluating the training and development of their staff and most of the book has been written at a level which should aid their understanding. This reflects my view that the ideas which people hold will largely determine the questions which they ask. These in turn will be related to the definitions which they are using.

In tracing the development of my ideas, looking at both theoretical and practical contributions, I am hoping to offer readers a framework in which to conceptualize their own knowledge and experience. This should make it possible for the reader to go back into the organizational context and ask different questions. Asking different questions is the first step in promoting the process of change.

PART ONE

Evaluating the training process

Introduction

The main thrust of this part of the book is that the processes by which training is designed and delivered can be evaluated against examples of good practice. Any process is made up of steps and, if it is systematic, each of these will arise logically from the model on which it is based. It is therefore worth while starting at this basic level and looking at the underlying model of any training activity. Models of training have different assumptions and are suitable for different purposes. Some models encourage discourse and assume that useful learning takes place as a result of interaction with others who have greater or, perhaps, different experience. Some are based on the principle that successful job performance is judged by the assessment of levels of skill and thus the function of training becomes to improve individual skills. Other models focus on improved effectiveness in the organizational context. It must surely be worth considering whether the model on which a training activity is based is consistent with the purpose. Examination of the literature and experience of practice suggests that very few trainers actually do this.

Training needs can be identified at organizational as well as individual levels. If the training is to be embedded in an organizational context, it would seem relevant for the identification process to take account of both levels and to try to balance the need for development of individuals with the requirements of the organization. Experience indicates that many trainers feel that their contribution is at the individual level. We will suggest that they might have more influence within the organization if they also consider the higher level.

The way in which trainees are selected, and the extent to which they as individuals are likely to be able to use the new skills or knowledge in their work, are clearly crucial to the success of the programme in terms of improved organizational effectiveness. Selecting trainees on a 'remedial' basis because they are judged to lack certain skills will logically lead to certain kinds of training process. Developmental activities should imply quite different processes, with more emphasis on work-based assignments and less on off the job courses.

The delivery of the programme itself is usually assessed against criteria of 'how well it went' seen from the perspective of the trainees as well as the tutors. There are more sophisticated ways of looking at the process during the programme and these are worth considering as they add information to the basic reaction level of assessment.

If what is learned during training is to result in different ways of performing the job, then some thought must be given to the transfer process. The process of transfer can start in the training, with the use of action planning and focusing on the utility of the learning, but it is often the case that, for effective transfer, the supervisor or line manager will need to be involved. The model which many trainers are using precludes their close contact with line managers and thus their ability to influence the quality of the transfer. Other models require close contact with line managers and, where transfer of training is thought to be a problem, these might be more suitable.

We will discuss these issues one by one and then, at the end of this part of the book, attempt to integrate them into a strategy for evaluating by examining processes.

1 Models of training

The individual training model

Training of individuals has its origin in craft apprenticeships where, over a period of some years, a young person learned to imitate the skills of his master. The learning model in use here was an ancient one based upon Socratic discourse, but with some hand–eye skills learned by the method of demonstration followed by practice followed by further demonstration. Training for trades and technical training in general has been greatly influenced by this tradition of teaching skills to individuals in the belief that they will later find a use for them. The model which is in use here looks like Figure 1.1.

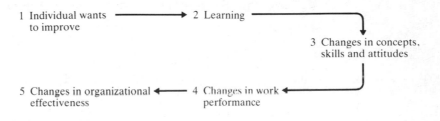

Figure 1.1 *Individual training model*

The focus is on individuals and the process is one of encouraging them to learn something said to be useful and then expecting them to find uses for the learning. This echoes the process of education in our schools and concentrates on only the first two parts of our definition of training. In attempting to evaluate training based on this model, it is sometimes very difficult to identify changes in work performance. With most forms of technical training, where the equipment used in training is very similar to that in the workplace, the changes in skills levels achieved during training will usually transfer quite easily into the job (provided there is an opportunity to practise them there). The model is, however, being used for other forms of training. Since the 1950s, it has become more and more necessary to train managers and supervisors as well as blue collar workers. With most supervisory and management training, the work situation does not closely resemble that simulated in the training and the changes achieved in the training programme are not necessarily reflected in changes in work performance. The latter will often mean changing the ways in which things are done within the organization and the model shown in Figure 1.1 is inappropriate for that purpose. As Katz and Kahn (1978) point out, attempts to change parts of organizations by using models like this have: 'a long history of theoretical inadequacy and practical failure' (1978, p658). The logic of this approach is that, as organizations are made up of individuals, it must be possible to change the organization by changing the members. This is, however, a great simplification of organizational reality. An organization will have objectives, priorities and policies. It will also have a structure and accepted ways of doing things. All of these situational factors will have some effect on shaping the behaviour of members of the organization within their work. Often the 'changed' individual is not able to change these situational factors.

It is worth while investigating this further as it is crucial to an under-standing of why training sometimes fails to have any effect. The work context can be represented as an interaction between the situation and the people in it (see Figure 1.2). If this interaction is not as effective as it might be, then changing the people by training might be considered as a way of improving things. However, this will only be successful if the people are sufficiently autonomous to change the interaction and thus the work situation. This might be the case where people are trained to use a piece of equipment like a keyboard or a lathe, but there is no reason to assume that it is the case with a supervisory problem. Other factors affect the situation and they may have more influence over the way in which the work is done than the skills of the people.

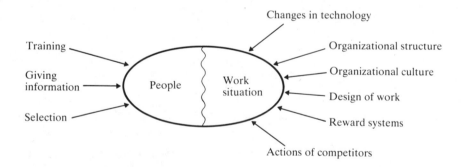

Figure 1.2   *Changing the way the work is done*

Such factors as the structure of the organization (who reports to whom, how many levels, and whether people can communicate horizontally), the culture (in what spirit people relate to each other, to what extent is individuality valued), the design of the work (the extent to which this is frustrating or stress-inducing), and whether good performance is actually rewarded (by recognition, praise, and promotion, as well as financially) will all affect the job situation. It will often be necessary to change some of these and to train the people as their effect on the interaction may be more powerful than the ability of the individuals to innovate in the job.

A distinction is being drawn here between training and giving information. The latter is a method which is widely used for changing the 'people' side of the interaction. At its most basic this may be feedback on organizational performance and an indication of how far this falls short of expectations, but there are many more sophisticated forms. Some, like management briefings and job induction programmes, are usually funded from the training department budget. It should also be noted that changing the people by selecting different people to fill key appointments or regrouping people into teams where more co-operation and less conflict is likely, might be a more effective method than training the people who are in the post.

Increased effectiveness model

We can see that changing the performance of people in the job is rather more complicated than Figure 1.1 would suggest. In order to think this through we need to consider a model which is based on changing effectiveness rather than on educating individuals. A possible model is offered in Figure 1.3. The process starts in a part of the organization with a decision about what level of effectiveness is desirable. The second stage is to define criteria by which changes towards the more desirable state can be measured, i.e. 'How will we know if we are getting there?'. In defining the resources necessary (stage three of the model), aspects of the job situation other than the skills of the people will be considered and it may be that changing some of these will achieve the desired improvements without training. If training is thought to be necessary, it is delivered, and the extent to which any learning is useful will be monitored by changes in job performance not, as is usually the case with the model in Figure 1.1, by changes measured during the training.

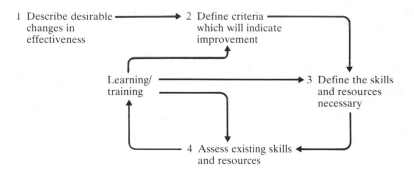

Figure 1.3 *Increased effectiveness model*

This model is much more appropriate for the kind of work where people have some discretion about what they do or the ability to negotiate priorities.

Considering the organizational context when using a model like this can have significant benefits. In a study reported by McGarrell (1984), induction training of new employees was redesigned to prepare them for the social context of the job and for the frustrations and opportunities of learning on the job. They also learned how their contribution would fit into their part of the organization and into the organization as a whole. The loss of people by leaving during the three months induction period dropped by 70 per cent and this gave a benefit–cost ratio of 8:1.

On the other hand, ignoring the organizational context can be expensive. Sykes (1962) described a training programme in which all 97 supervisors in an organization were trained to be more participative in their management style. The values instilled during training were not those of the management of the organization and the supervisors were frustrated in their attempts to introduce participative management in the workplace. Within a year 19 of the supervisors had left and another 25 were actively seeking other employment. The training, although efficient in changing the attitudes of the supervisors, was not effective in contributing to organizational goals.

The training process as a systematic cycle

Training is usually planned using a process like that in Figure 1.4. This is often said to be a 'systems approach' to training, implying that the subsystems within the cycle interact. We prefer the term 'systematic' as it is our experience that the process being described goes from step to step in a logical fashion but the subsystems rarely interact nor do they interact with other organizational subsystems like job design, reward systems or organizational restructuring. The result of this is often efficient rather than effective training because the training objectives, once defined, become synonymous with the training need and the training subsystem becomes the closed cycle which is shown in Figure 1.5. In order to be open to the organizational context the training should be evaluated against the need originally identified, in the part of the organization where it existed. This is not often done.

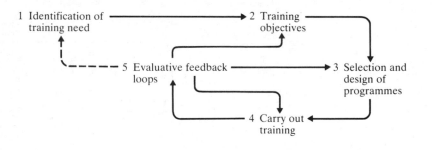

Figure 1.4 *The systematic training cycle*

Training as organizational change

A quite different cycle is suggested by considering training as a way of enhancing organizational effectiveness. The process starts with an analysis of the existing situation as suggested in Figure 1.3. The needs identified will be phrased in terms of new work practices which will enhance the effectiveness of one particular part of the organization. The management of that part of the organization must be involved at all stages and be committed to changing organizational structures or practices which conflict with the new practices which are being introduced. In almost every case this will imply that the managers are involved in the design and

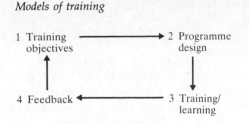

Figure 1.5 *Training as a closed loop*

delivery of the training. They will also be responsible for encouraging the new behaviours in the workplace by appraising performance and coaching or supervising as necessary to ensure that the learning becomes incorporated in standard work practices.

It should be noted that this model is profoundly different to that shown in Figure 1.1. The intention is the same, i.e. to change the way in which individuals work, but now the new behaviours are embedded in the organizational context. In the earlier model they were encouraged in a training context and it was hoped that individuals would apply them in their work. We suggest that you consider these two models as possible ways of changing part of the organizational culture, of trying to achieve a more participative management style. Would training individual managers and supervisors and returning them to an unsuspecting workplace be likely to succeed? Would the procedure suggested by Figure 1.6 be more or less likely to succeed?

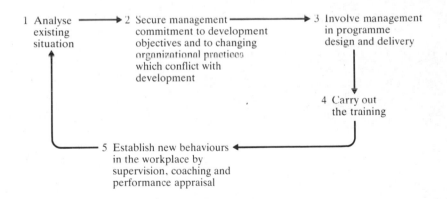

Figure 1.6 *Training as organizational change*

Summary

The model of training which is most prevalent has developed from educational practice and the intention is to teach an individual how to carry out some part of a well-defined job. Where the information and/or skills practice given are closely matched to a job which is not changing, this may be an adequate model. Where it is intended that the training given should help the individual to change the job situation, this model is often not appropriate as it assumes that the individual has sufficient autonomy to change the way in which 'things are done' in part of the organization.

If the intention is to change the effectiveness of the individual or of part of the organization, a different model may be more appropriate. This is controlled by measuring changes in criteria of effectiveness rather than by input of hours of teaching. The model is one of organizational change combined with learning rather than the more traditional approach of training the individual.

2 Identification of training needs

The accurate identification of the training needs of an organization is crucial to its success and development. However, theory does little to assist those who face this difficult task. It is not simply a matter of deciding on the location, scope and magnitude of the needs. Priorities need to be set and linked to those of other functions within the organization as well as to the organization as a whole.

Three levels of analysis

The most influential text on training needs analysis is that of McGehee and Thayer (1961). They argue that training needs analysis requires much more than 'armchair cerebration' and suggest analysis at three levels—the organization, job and person. Although the needs analysis will usually consist of three distinct investigations, McGehee and Thayer argue that these should be interrelated so that they build on each other to produce a complete training needs statement.

- Analysis at the *organizational level* is used to determine where training can and should be used. The focus is the total enterprise and the analysis will look at things like the organizational objectives, the pool of skills presently available, indices of effectiveness and the organizational climate.
- Analysis at the *job level* involves collecting data about a particular job or group of jobs. The analysis will determine what standards are required and what knowledge, skills and attitudes are required in order to achieve these standards.
- The focus of *person analysis* is how well a particular employee is carrying out the various tasks which are necessary for successful performance.

Organizational analysis

Training and development is a subsystem of the organization and has its own inputs from the organization and outputs to the organization. If this interaction is to result in increased organizational effectiveness, then it is clear that priorities for training needs must be related to organizational goals. This implies that the training plan should be constructed in the same context as the business plan and be closely related to it. Hussey's survey (1985) of British companies suggests that only about a third of them actually do this. Most managers felt that training objectives should be tailored to the individual rather than to corporate needs. Hussey argues that training should not be for the individual in the hope that it will benefit the organization; training should be for the benefit of the organization as this will benefit the individuals in it. Thus training objectives, especially those for management development, should be reviewed regularly by top management and particularly whenever a change in direction or emphasis is planned. It appears that, in the USA, the likelihood of this happening is increasing. Bolt's survey (1987) shows that between 1983 and 1986 there was an increase in top management commitment to management training and development and that: 'senior corporate management is expecting the training profession to deliver results and to contribute materially to implementing corporate strategies and achieving business objectives'.

McGehee and Thayer recommend a number of sources of data to support the analysis of needs at organizational level:

1 Organizational goals and objectives will provide targets for the various functions within the organization. Some of these will imply changes in performance standards and these may have training implications.
2 The manpower plan will predict gaps caused by retirements, promotions and turnover. This provides a demographic basis for identifying training (and selection) required to fill the gaps.
3 The skills pool is an inventory of knowledge and skills held within the organization. The maintenance of this will indicate training needs. It is also possible to predict some of the skills which will be required in the future and which are not, at present, available.
4 Organizational climate indices like turnover, absenteeism, short-term sickness, attitude surveys, grievances and strikes, will sometimes indicate training needs as well as altering some aspects of the work situation.
5 Efficiency indices like costs of labour and materials, quality of product, equipment utilization, cost of distribution, waste, machine downtime, late deliveries, repairs, or customer complaints, may indicate a shortfall in performance which can be improved by training.
6 Requests by line management or surveys of their opinions are often used to build up the training plan.
7 There is also often a training implication when new systems or new equipments are introduced.

Aspects of organizational effectiveness

The linking of training to the organizational context in which the work is done is fundamental to this level of analysis. One way of doing this, which we have found useful, is to talk regularly to managers about how they conceptualize 'effectiveness'. This method is based on critical incident analysis and the procedure is as follows:

• Target a function within the organization and arrange interviews with a representative sample of line managers and supervisors. Arrange to see the more senior ones first.
• Discuss aspects of organizational effectiveness with each member of your sample. Ask each to describe one or two incidents when things were going particularly well or badly; how the incident developed, what criteria were being used to judge 'well' or 'badly', what was the result of the incident in organizational terms. Use something like Fig-

ure 2.1 to classify the types of organizational effectiveness being used (and perhaps also offer the managers this list to prompt them). This framework for conceptualizing organizational effectiveness is derived from the work of Cameron (1980) and it is discussed more fully in a later section when we examine how to assess changes in effectiveness as a result of training.

Achieving goals
- Increased product/service quality
- Increased output
- Increased productivity

Increasing resourcefulness
- Increased share of the market
- Increased employee versatility
- Moving into new markets

Satisfying customers
- Improved organizational (or functional image)
- Reduced complaints/returned material
- Increased proportion of on-time deliveries

Improving internal processes
- Increased group cohesiveness
- Increased quality of supervision
- Help resolve departmental boundary problems
- Increasing managers' ability to set realistic and tangible objectives for their departments

---

Figure 2.1 *Aspects of organizational effectiveness*
Source: adapted from Cameron, 1980

As a result of this discussion try to understand the key results and priorities for a particular manager or supervisor. Discuss to what extent the present training provision helps with these key areas of effectiveness and also discuss whether another form of training activity might help.

An integration of the ideas generated in these interviews should give a clear view of what training and development might be able to do to improve the effectiveness of the particular function. This should be fed back to the senior managers in the function and the objectives for the training agreed. There will also be a need to commit the senior managers to supporting the training by increased supervision or coaching and/or changing some of the work practices which are associated with low effectiveness.

Job data analysis

At the job data level of analysis it is necessary to discover what tasks need to be performed in order to do the job, how they should be performed and thus what needs to be learned in order to perform well. McGehee and Thayer offer a number of techniques for carrying out such an analysis:

1 Job descriptions will give an outline of the job and list typical duties and responsibilities. For some jobs these will change each year in response to setting new priorities.

2 Job specifications are more detailed than job descriptions and should give a complete list of tasks. They may also include standards for judging satisfactory performance in the important tasks.

3 Performance standards are usually phrased as objectives for the job and the targets or standards by which these will be judged.

4 Actually doing the job is very effective for specific tasks, but has obvious limitations in jobs where there are long gaps between performance and outcomes.

5 Job observation or work sampling might also be used to look in detail at particular parts of the job.

Asking the job holder and the supervisor about the job is also a method suggested by McGehee and Thayer. This has been developed by the Armed Forces into a complex analysis by sending to all incumbents and their supervisors questionnaires asking about frequency, importance and difficulty of various tasks which might be part of the job. The answers

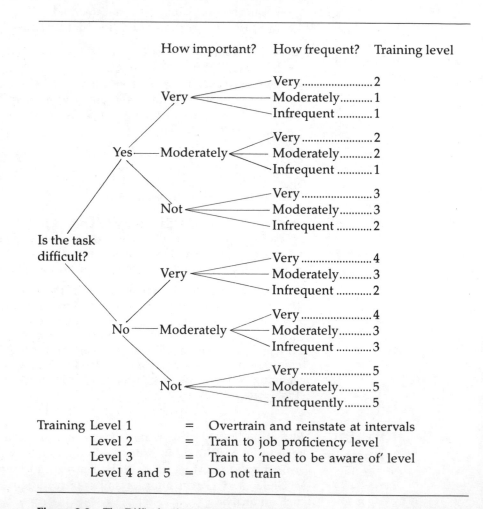

How important?	How frequent?	Training level
	Very	2
Very	Moderately	1
	Infrequent	1
	Very	2
Yes — Moderately	Moderately	2
	Infrequent	1
	Very	3
Not	Moderately	3
	Infrequent	2
	Very	4
Very	Moderately	3
	Infrequent	2
	Very	4
No — Moderately	Moderately	3
	Infrequent	3
	Very	5
Not	Moderately	5
	Infrequently	5

Is the task difficult?

Training Level 1	=	Overtrain and reinstate at intervals
Level 2	=	Train to job proficiency level
Level 3	=	Train to 'need to be aware of' level
Level 4 and 5	=	Do not train

Figure 2.2 *The Difficulty/frequency/importance matrix*

are analysed, usually by a computer programme called CODAP (Comprehensive Data Analysis Programme) which clusters the tasks, and this gives a complete specification of the job or, more usually, of a group of related jobs forming a trade structure. Training programmes are then designed based on decision trees like that in Figure 2.2.

Where training programmes already exist, it is possible to estimate the relevance to successful job performance of the various topics covered. Ford and Wroten (1984) describe a method and its application for evaluating a training programme for police patrol officers. Subject matter experts (i.e. patrol officers, sergeants and police officers from other cities) independently rated the importance of knowledge, skills and attitudes learned in training for successful job performance. The extent to which each area of knowledge, aspect of skill or attitude was necessary for satisfactory performance was then calculated as a 'content validity ratio'. The training curriculum was then examined and the amount of time devoted to each topic linked to the content validity.

Goldstein (1986) has suggested an alternative method of correlating job analysis information with the amount of time devoted to topics during training. Faley and Sandstrom (1985) describe a method of assessing the relevance of the content of a training programme by using the Position Analysis Questionnaire (PAQ). Training programme analysts used the PAQ to analyse the programme as if it were a job. Job incumbents also used the PAQ to analyse the job itself. The profile comparison identified those areas which the programme either over- or under-emphasized.

All three methods have the strength of firmly defining the training requirement in terms of job performance. It sounds rather obvious but it may be necessary. In my experience, trainers have a tendency to concentrate on what they enjoy teaching (or what they believe the trainees will enjoy learning) and the training content can drift away from the job requirement. In one particular programme which we evaluated, half of the theoretical content was not relevant to successful job performance.

Person analysis

At the individual level of analysis, the intention is to assess performance levels against those required in the job. Theoretically, a training programme can then be designed for each individual to close the gap between present and desired levels of performance. McGehee and Thayer offer a long list of techniques by which individual training needs can be identified. These include the following:

- Performance appraisal which identifies weaknesses and areas for improvement as well as strengths.
- Observation and work sampling, or testing of knowledge and skills required in the job.
- Interviews and questionnaires.
- Devising situations like role plays, case studies, business games and in-baskets. Recently these have often been combined in assessment centres where the main purpose is identifying development needs rather than selection.

A word of caution ought to be introduced here. We are using the word 'need' to mean an observable discrepancy in performance produced by the lack of skill and *not* to mean a job holder's expression of preference for or interest in a particular programme. It is also worth noting that a performance deficiency does not necessarily imply a training need. For instance, Mager and Pipe (1970) recommend the algorithm in Figure 2.3. This should remind us that job situation factors like organizational culture, structure and reward systems may be more powerful controllers of job behaviour than the abilities of the individuals in the job.

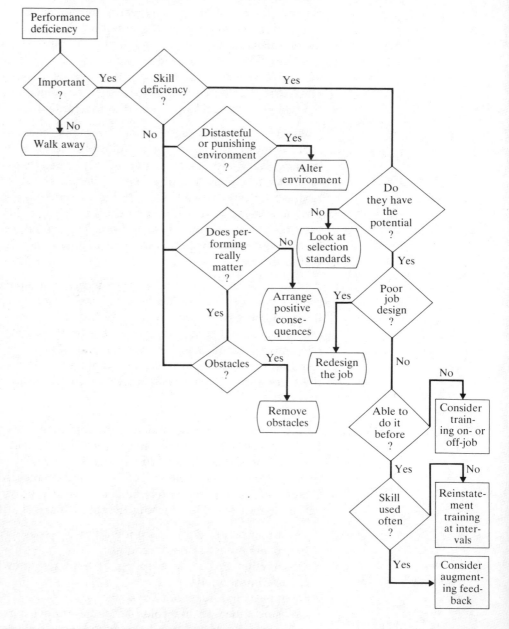

Figure 2.3 *Performance deficiency training problem?*
Source: adapted from Mager, R.F. and Pipe, P., 1970

Rowland, in 1970, reported on a survey of 4 000 managers in which he asked, 'Why do subordinates fail?' The most popular answers given are shown below, listed in order of frequency:

They do not know what they are supposed to do
They do not know how to do it
They do not know why they should do it
There are obstacles beyond their control
They do not think it will work
They think that their way is better
They were not motivated (or poor attitude)
They were incapable of doing it (or poor skills)
There was insufficient time to do it
They were working on the wrong priority items
They thought that they *were* doing it
Poor management
Personal problems

An interesting development in person analysis for managerial jobs has been the recent emphasis on observable behaviour rather than abstract qualities. This usually takes the form of defining the 'competencies' which are important for successful performance in a particular job and the appraisal of the incumbent against these competencies. (Examples of 'competencies' are: developing people, analysing problems, representing part of the organization, chairing meetings, resolving disputes, developing new procedures, making decisions, etc. Many lists are available and the key results areas of most jobs can be defined in less than a dozen competencies.) Where this is done as a joint exercise between a manager and his or her supervisor it usually results in a statement of development needs. Where the supervisor does it alone it more often results in a judgement.

Integration of the three levels of analysis

Training needs analyses often concentrate on the person analysis level and neglect the links with organizational goals which are necessary to ensure that the training is effective in advancing the cause of the company. One way of avoiding this is to carry out the analyses in a sequential way as suggested in Figure 2.4.

The process starts by examining the performance of the organization or of one part of it. If this suggests a possible training need, then the group of jobs in the area under review is examined. This may lead to an analysis of the individuals in posts to discover whether training is likely to change the current level of performance into one which is nearer the optimal level for the job. At all three levels of analysis alternative solutions are considered in the way suggested by Mager and Pipe (Figure 2.3).

An alternative method for integrating training needs is to start from the business plan and cascade objectives down through the organization. An example of good practice was given by a petro-chemicals company with which we were involved as consultants. First the chief executive

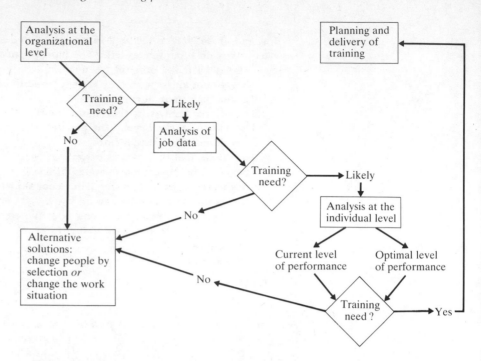

Figure 2.4   *Training needs assessment model*
Source: adapted from Vintor, Clark and Seybolt, 1983

decided his objectives for the coming year. He held a half-day meeting with his general managers to explain his objectives and then to allow each of them to develop their own objectives and share these with the other general managers. This formed the basis of the business plan.

Next, each general manager cascaded objectives down through their part of the company by organizing between four and six half-day sessions in sequence so that the higher order objectives were broken down and interpreted. At each level some negotiation of the objectives was necessary in order to incorporate the realities at that level. The result of this process was that each of the departments and indeed each individual manager had negotiated their objectives for the next year and knew how these integrated vertically right up to those of the chief executive. (The sequence of top–down was important; in one part of the company it got out of phase and it was noticeable that here the objectives were not integrated and there was not the same sense of purpose.)

The next phase was to incorporate these objectives into the annual appraisal by each manager agreeing with his or her supervisor the targets which represented the key results areas. Each key result area was analysed (by discussion between manager and supervisor) for the competencies required to achieve it, then the training needs were identified in terms of competencies thought desirable but not well-developed. The training department was thus able to collect lists of competencies to be developed and, by clustering these, produce a training plan.

The data base derived from this has produced information for job descriptions, recruitment and bonus payments. It has also produced a profile of the managers in the company in terms of skills available (defined as competencies). This was examined and discussed at Board level in order to establish longer-term development activities required for the management group to meet future challenges.

The process has proved to be very powerful in motivating the managers —they can see exactly how their contributions fit into the overall effort and they are convinced that the company cares about their development. It is now being repeated for a second year and is likely to become a standard process which is central to the whole human resource management of the company.

Perhaps this is a good place to think about how the training needs are identified in *your* organization.

1 What methods are being used to identify needs at the organizational level?
2 What methods at the job level?
3 What methods at the person level?
4 How well are the three levels integrated? Which predominates, and why?
5 How well is training linked to the business plan? What could be done to strengthen this link? Who could do it? What *can you* do?

Latham (1988) states that:

'Organizational support for training should be operationally defined as the extent to which training objectives are linked to organizational objectives, the extent to which the training objectives change as soon as there is a change in the organization's strategic emphasis, and the extent to which training progress is viewed together with the progress made in achieving the business plan.'

What is the extent of the support for training in *your* organization?

3 Sequencing learning experiences

Training in its organizational context

Having decided that a need can be met with some form of training, and having defined the changes in performances against which the training will be evaluated, the next area which needs attention is the sequencing of the learning. The word 'learning' is chosen deliberately to emphasize that delivering training is not the same as actually learning while taking part in the activity. The first model of training which we looked at (Figure 1.1) is essentially an input model, as the changes in performance are expected rather than built into the process. To put this model into its organizational context gives us something like Figure 3.1.

1 Selection to attend training →	2 Briefing and preparation	→ 3 Becoming committed to learning
		↓
		4 Learning
		↓
7 Transfer of learning ←	6 Return to work ←	5 Preparing for transfer of learning back to the job

(The vertical line between stages 2 and 3, and between 5 and 6, is intended to represent the distance between the job situation and the training activity)

Figure 3.1 *Training in its organizational context*
Source: adapted from Berger, 1977

Pre-activity learner support

Selection

We have discussed above, at some length, the selection of the right people for a particular training activity. Here are some questions which I would ask you to consider in relation to selection in your own organization:

1 Do you question participants at the beginning of a training event about why they have come?

2 What proportion attend only because someone else had been booked for the training, but could not come?

3 How many attend because it is their turn to do 'some' training this year?

4 What proportion have asked for this programme because they know of someone else who enjoyed it?

5 How many participants know what kind of person is most likely to benefit from the particular learning which is being offered?

6 How often do you send someone back because the training is not appropriate for them?

7 How well is selection done in your organization?

The training can be efficient in doing what it sets out to do. However, it cannot be effective if the wrong people are attending.

Briefing and preparation

The second phase of the model (Figure 3.1) implies that, before the training takes place, the developmental objectives should be established between the person who is to learn something and the person who is nominating him or her. Most adult learning is motivated by attempts to reach goals which the individual has set (for example, see Locke *et al.*, 1981). In order to tap this source of motivation, it is clear that the participants must be aware of the objectives and to some extent identify with them as personal objectives. What form does the pre-programme briefing take in your organization?

• Who does the briefing?
• Are learning objectives clarified and agreed?
• Do the supervisors/managers understand them?
• Was any pre-programme activity required? Was it carried out?

The broken line between phases 2 and 3 in Figure 3.1 imply moving from the job to the training. If nothing happens at phase 2, which is often the case, then at phase 3, in the training event, the first day is spent trying to commit people to learning objectives. If the training is done on the job, this is not too serious, but if it is off the job, there is a danger that the objectives set will be personal development or therapy objectives which have little to do with improving performance in the job. On an interpersonal skills programme, have you ever looked at the flip charts which adorn the walls and which state, 'My objectives for the week are. . .'? Do they reflect learning which will improve job performance?

The sequence of the programme

The learning situations themselves should be sequenced so that people can use various styles of learning and integrate them into a meaningful whole. A useful model to consider is that of Kolb (1984) which is based on adults learning from their experience. Figure 3.2 illustrates the cycle of learning.

The theory requires activity in all four stages for effective learning. This implies that there should be some concrete experience, with the learners involving themselves fully and openly, and some reflective observation, with the learners helped to step back and reflect upon the experience.

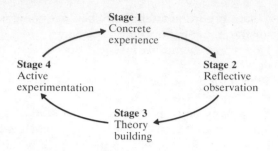

Figure 3.2   *The Kolb cycle of learning*

These two stages should be followed by a phase when they are helped
to integrate their observations into a logically sound framework, i.e. they
alter their general theory of 'how things like this work'. The final stage
is to put them into active experimentation so that they can test their
theories and use them as bases for decision-making and problem-solving.

Few people are equally strong in all these phases so the learning situation should offer more support in those stages in which they are
weakest. This is a tall order for a designer of training programmes. It is
not too difficult to set up experiences and to assist the learners to analyse
what they have experienced, but to encourage them to incorporate these
experiences into their way of thinking is often beyond the ability of the
trainers. Testing their learning in other, similar situations takes time
(more time than is usually available in training events), so this phase is
usually left to chance, i.e. the hope that they will try it at work.

A better process would be to ensure that they can try out the ideas in
the work situation and have the opportunity to discuss the results with
someone, i.e. action learning.

During the learning, some emphasis should be placed on examining
what is being learned for utility back on the job, and plans should be
made for transferring the learning. Usually this will involve an action
plan which anticipates some of the organizational constraints on introducing change.

If all the first five phases in Figure 3.1 have been done properly, then it
should be possible to return to work and transfer the learning. Often,
however, the learning 'burns off' on re-entry because no one in the
workplace carries out a debriefing and offers support. The most common experience is to be greeted by, 'Had a good time? We have been
busy while you have been away, but we have kept some of it for you;
it's all in your in-tray'. On emerging from the in-tray two weeks later,
the training programme seems to be a historical event.

One area of training, that of interpersonal skills, has a particularly poor
record in transferring. It is worth looking at the model in order to isolate why this should be so. It is a confused area because many trainers
are actually trying to change *attitudes* but are calling its *skills* training.
Underlying this is a belief that if peoples' attitudes are changed this will
lead to behaviour changes, i.e. improved skills, but there is not much
evidence to support it.

Psychomotor skills training does transfer well and it is probably because it has the following outline:

- Isolate critical skills from job samples and specify what they look like in some detail
- Demonstrate the skill, break it down into phases and practise it, giving feedback throughout the exercise to narrow the gap between actual and desired performance
- Transfer the skill to the workplace and give further feedback until the level achieved in training reaches operational standard

Two aspects of this are crucial to the success of the training:

- The feedback in training must be similar to that of the job situation, i.e. high environmental fidelity is essential
- The amount of transfer is directly proportional to the number of elements common to both training and job situations

The model usually used in interpersonal skills training ignores important aspects of this skills model:

- Very generalized sets of behaviours are called skills (e.g. 'communication')
- The feedback given is artificial and nothing like that available in the work situation (i.e. no environmental fidelity)
- The learning activity takes place off the job and there are very few elements common to both the training and the job (one of the crucial elements, for instance, is the actual people one has to work with)

One successful method of training people in interpersonal skills was developed by Goldstein and Sorcher (1974). They adopted the principles of social learning theory and applied them to a programme for training supervisors in behaviours like:

1 orientating a new employee
2 giving on-job training
3 motivating the poor performer
4 handling discrimination complaints
5 conducting a performance review

The training sessions were of two-hour duration off the job and were structured as follows:

1 The importance of the topic to the success of the job was emphasized by the trainers and agreed by the supervisors
2 A video was shown which portrayed a model effectively handling the type of situation to be examined
3 Key points were drawn from the modelling
4 Group discussion took place on the effectiveness and relevance of the modelled behaviours
5 Role playing by the supervisors with feedback from the group

The supervisors then went back to the job and reported in the next session, held two weeks later, whether they had encountered the situation and how they had responded to it. It is essential that both the application to the actual situation and reporting back for discussion of outcomes are incorporated into the training process. Without both of them the chances of successful transfer are slight. Where, as in this method, attention has been paid to transfer, improvements have been noted.

The training reported by Goldstein and Sorcher was evaluated in terms of productivity levels in the work areas for which the four supervisors were responsible. These showed an improvement in three out of the four areas. There were decreases in productivity in the fourth area and also in all of the areas of responsibility of the four supervisors who had been selected as 'controls' and were not trained.

The book by Goldstein and Sorcher is an excellent text, unique in training literature in that it starts from a thoroughly researched theory, adapts it to a field situation, and tests it. It has led to a number of studies further investigating behavioural role modelling as a training technique. The best of these to date has been Saari's Masters degree project, published as Latham and Saari (1979). Faced with the problem of training 100 supervisors in an organization, they decided to follow the same training procedure as Goldstein and Sorcher (indeed they used the models recorded on video by Sorcher). Not all the foremen could be trained at once, so groups were selected for early training and those to be trained later were used (unknowingly) as controls. The design of the study was:

Test 1	Train	Test 2	Train	Test 3	
Gp A	A	A	—	A	n = 20
Gp B	—	B	B	B	n = 20
Similar baseline		Expect A better		Expect similar	

The testing was done at three levels, those of 'learning', 'behaviour' and 'results'. Learning was assessed by a test of knowledge of the key aspects of the behaviour thought likely to be successful in the critical incidents trained. Behaviour was assessed by observation and reports from managers and results from measures of productivity in the sections for which the supervisors were responsible. The training was a great success.

Behaviour modelling has become popular as a method of management and supervisor training. Mayer and Russell (1987) were able to review 14 studies conducted in field settings. The research reveals that trainees *react* positively to behaviour modelling training and also that it is effective at the *learning* level. The evidence concerning the effectiveness of it in influencing *performance* is more equivocal.

Explanations put forward to account for this variable transfer of learning back to the job usually include descriptions of unreceptive work cultures. This may, however, be too simple. The theoretical basis for transfer of social learning is derived from the work of Bandura (1977, 1986). Bandura would argue that cognitive mediating variables play a part in transfer and that the most important of these is 'self-efficacy'. This is defined as a self-judgement of how able one is to successfully carry through a course of action required to deal with a particular situation.

The level of this will depend not only upon perceived mastery of knowledge and skills, but also upon the perception of the work situation. The implication here is that there should be some support available in the work situation to enhance self-efficacy for those in whom it is relatively low; those in whom self-efficacy is relatively high will be able to use the skills learned.

This returns us to the point made earlier, that high environmental fidelity is needed in order to achieve high levels of transfer in skills training, but it goes further in encouraging us to think of the developing manager as increasing in self-efficacy, i.e. increasing knowledge and skills and also the perception of being confident in using them.

A quite different theoretical approach is described in the excellent book on interpersonal skills training by Rackham and Morgan (1977) who treated the learning process as information processing (stage by stage reduction of uncertainty by use of feedback). The categories of behaviour to be learned were selected on the basis of their having a critical bearing on the effectiveness of job behaviour. The training was intended to provide a vocabulary to allow the participants to identify categories of behaviour and to give feedback to reduce the discrepancy between the actual use of these categories and their perception of how frequently they used them. The feedback was given on samples of behaviour at work, recorded by an observer.

The key aspect of all this is the integration between tracking of behaviour change and training. There is a continual cycle of evaluation, feedback and training leading to further evaluation feedback and training. This is a true skills model and Rackham and Morgan describe a number of successful applications of behaviour analysis in training. Their book represents a very impressive body of work.

Patrick, Michael and Moore (1986) describe six types of learning: learning facts, discriminations, concepts, rules, procedures, and problem-solving. The categories are largely based on Gagne's work (1970) and reflect behavioural research on learning. The course design proceeds from:

- identifying the types of learning required
- selecting a suitable method for each type
- sequencing the programme from the lowest to the highest type of learning required

Each of these three approaches—behaviour modelling described by Goldstein and Sorcher, behaviour analysis used by Rackham and Morgan and designing learning in the way suggested by Patrick, Michael and Moore—has the strength of being founded on a sound theoretical base which gives some unity and purpose to the design of the programme rather than the *ad hoc* pragmatism which is more typical of trainers. Some unity to the design will increase the likelihood of learning and also its transfer to the job. Programmes which are made up of a collection of learning situations, each used because it has proved interesting in the past, usually do not have a unifying design and the learning does not develop in a way which aids transfer.

It is possible, and often useful, to look at the delivery of the programme in some detail. As well as the overall course structure which we have been discussing, it might be worth examining the use of objectives, the methods and media, and the use of feedback. Questions which might be posed are listed in Figure 3.3.

Objectives

- Have the tutorial staff access to a copy of the current objectives?
- Are the objectives clear and unambiguous?
- Does achievement of the objectives mean all training needs are met or is some on-job training required?
- To what extent are the tutors familiar with the trainee's learning objectives? How are they taking these into account?

Course structure

- On what principles is the course structured?
- Is there a satisfactory balance between practice, reflection and theory input?
- How satisfactory is the duration of the course and the length of the working day?
- Does the balance of the course reflect the different degrees of importance attached to the objectives?

Methods and media

- On what basis have the methods been chosen?
- Are optimal methods being used, given the characteristics of the learners?
- Do methods and media provide variety and encourage learning?
- What is the quality and readability of handouts, computer-based training material and training aids?

Evaluative feedback

- What form of assessment of progress is being used during the programme?
- Is each assessment method reliable and timely?
- How is feedback given to the trainees?
- How is feedback used by the tutors? Is there enough flexibility to allow for individual remedial work, etc?
- Are summarizing and consolidating sessions built into the programme?
- Are evaluative reports written on courses? To whom are they sent? Is any action taken as a result of these reports?

Figure 3.3 *Questions about a programme*

Figure 3.3. lists more questions on the use of evaluative feedback during the programme than on any other area. This reflects my view that learning is a cyclical process and, therefore, that feedback is necessary at each stage in order to evaluate how present performance differs from that desired. This feedback should be given before new learning takes place. An end-of-course discussion is usually too late to allow for this. (A useful review of the various uses of feedback is given by Stammers and Patrick, 1975.)

Transfer of learning

As we can see in Figure 3.1, the final phase in the training cycle is the incorporation into normal work of new ways of thinking or carrying out tasks. Often this is left to the individual, the implication being that the individual has the motivation and the ability to introduce such changes. Looking at Figure 3.4, the assumption is that the people who have been trained can take the 'effective' route. Is this realistic? Attempts will have been made during training to focus on the utility of the learning and to produce action plans for the return to work. Clearly these must include analysis of situations which are likely to test the new learning and the consideration of strategies to enlist support and to deflect opposition. Temporary difficulties are to be expected and the intention must be to prevent these from becoming relapses into old behaviours.

Uses skills learned and copes → Sense of accomplishment → Increased likelihood of using the new behaviour = Effective transfer

Shortly after training, a risky situation occurs   Training activity

Tries to use new skills but cannot cope → Sense of lack of control → Increased likelihood of using the old behaviour = No transfer

Figure 3.4 *Using new skills in the workplace*

We are back in the area of self-efficacy here. People who judge themselves low have difficulty in coping with environmental demands. They imagine that potential difficulties are more formidable than is actually the case and they dwell on their personal deficiencies. People who are strong in self-efficacy focus on the demands of the situation and treat obstacles as a challenge. Self-efficacy has been found to increase when experience fails to support fears and when the skills learned help to master the situation which was felt to be threatening. Much of this is to do with ability to predict and manage perceived threats. How can we increase self-efficacy in a training programme?

- Maximize the similarity between the training situation and the job, if necessary by carrying out the training in phases with job experience interspersed.
- Provide a wide range of experience of what is being learned so that the principles can be applied to situations which do not exactly fit the

procedure. If we divide the material to be learned into three levels this implies spending some time on the 'analysis' level:

> 3 Analysis of situations to decide which procedures are
>   likely to be successful
>   ↑
> 2 Learning procedures or ways of carrying out tasks
>   ↑
> 1 Learning isolated pieces of information

- Ensure that what is being learned will be supported and rewarded in the workplace. There is clearly a role for the supervisor or manager here; he or she must be a party to the training and transfer.
- Goal-setting is important because without it people will have a poor basis for judging their progress. Clear measures of progress are essential for increasing self-efficacy, trainees should be deterred from setting very difficult goals as those who give up are often those who self-impose very high standards and then feel no sense of accomplishment because they fail to reach them.

One other major finding from the literature on transfer of training is worth noting here. Retention is especially difficult when there is a significant time delay between the learning and its application. This is not so serious where perceptual/motor skills are involved but it is serious where the skills are primarily based on cognitive/knowledge processes. Wetzel, Konoske and Montague (1983) have shown that these skills, based upon knowledge of procedures, can be subject to rapid and extensive loss in a few weeks. Another instance of this was described by Prophet (1976) who showed that psychomotor flight skills are retained for many months longer than procedural flight skills. Hagman and Rose (1983) reviewed the retention of on-job skills which were infrequently

---

This might be a good place to pause for thought. The problems raised by the transfer of training have encouraged many organizations to take training nearer to the workplace. We have already mentioned behaviour modelling and behaviour analysis where training in interpersonal skills and their application at work are integrated. There is also the whole field of action learning (see, for example, Pedler, 1983) where the transfer problem is avoided by using actual work problems as media for training. What is it like in your organization? How do you attempt to maximize transfer? Do you have any post-programme learner support?

1 What form does the post-programme briefing take?
2 Who does it?
3 Are action plans reviewed and priorities set?
4 What constraints are being put on the trainees' ability to apply the learning?
5 What support is available to close the gap between levels of achievement on the programme and competent job performance?
6 What changes are being achieved in terms of:
- **different individual performance levels?**
- **increased levels of organizational effectiveness?**

7 What criteria of effectiveness of training are being used?

practised, such as emergency procedures, and found that they often showed deterioration to the point of being problematic. It is common knowledge that emergency and safety procedures need reinstatement training at intervals. What the literature is telling us is that this is also true of things covered in management development programmes if the new ideas have not been applied fairly soon (probably within three months) after the learning experience.

4 The training function in its organizational context

Mapping training activities

A useful starting point for examining the fit between the training system and its organizational context is to make up matrices of the type suggested by Pepper (1984). The example shown in Figure 4.1 is intended to be a general case. Across the top of the matrix one enters the categories of people who make up the organization—say senior managers, middle managers, first-line managers/supervisors, operators, clerical staff. Down the side are various organizational processes.

	Senior mgt	Middle mgt	First-line mgt	Operators	Clerical staff
Induction for people joining					
Training on being promoted					
Changes of plant or equipment					
Changes in structure and procedures					
Maintenance of standards					
Maintenance of capabilities					
Changes in standards or legislation					

Figure 4.1 *A training opportunity matrix*
Source: adapted from Pepper, 1984

The matrix is drawn as a wallchart and mapped onto it are the training activities offered at present, in the recent past and in the near future. Any specific activity may be represented in more than one box of the matrix, either because different target groups are included or because different organizational processes are addressed. Looking closely at this matrix gives one a good feel for what types of programme are being provided and also what is *not* being provided. Questions can then be formulated to investigate the logic underlying this provision. In large organizations it will be necessary to draw up a separate matrix for each function; the requirements for production will not be the same as those for marketing, etc.

Some of the questions raised by the examination of the matrices are best answered by a survey within the functions. A suggested way of doing this is to discuss, with a sample of line managers and supervisors, the ways in which training could help to improve the effectiveness of that part of the organization for which they are responsible. We have already referred to this when we were thinking about identifying training needs at the organizational level and aspects of effectiveness were listed in Figure 2.1. We will return to this again in Part 2 when we are considering methods of measuring changes in levels of effectiveness.

A second aspect of mapping training activities involves looking at the various methods of delivery which are being used by the organization. To assist in doing this, the following questions might be useful:

- Which programmes are being run internally and which are being contracted out? On what grounds were the decisions made to run them in this way?
- What is the range of methods of delivery in use? Distance learning? Paper-based texts? Video packages? On-job? Team development? Learner-centred discovery? To what extent are these various methods appropriate for the topic and for the type of trainee?
- What investigations are being conducted into the use of new methods and technology? What aspects of learning effectiveness are being considered? Is user-acceptability being examined? Is anyone carrying out cost-effectiveness comparisons?
- To what extent is training devolved into the functions? How active are line managers in the training of their people?

Skills training versus career development?

The development of human resources within the organization will include selection, assessment of performance, estimation of potential and some form of career planning for individuals as well as the overall manpower planning for the future. Skills training should contribute to this process and should be integrated into the planning.

One way of integrating this is suggested by the consideration of corporate business plans at three levels: (1) strategic, (2) co-ordinative, and (3) operational (Katz and Khan, 1978).

1 *Strategic* plans are the concern of top management, have a long-term perspective and cover the whole organization.

2 *Co-ordinative* plans concern middle managers, have shorter time horizons and cover only a part of the organization (usually each function).
3 *Operational* plans concern junior managers and supervisors, are short-term and refer to only a small part of the organization.

These three levels can be related to the selection and development of staff in the organization:

- At the *strategic* level the requirement is to draw up plans for the development of management and workforce to enable the organization to change in desired directions.
- At the *co-ordinative* level the main requirement is to develop the experience of managers to ensure the supply of future middle and senior managers.
- At the *operational* level the emphasis should be on training people to improve their performance in their present jobs.

The priority given to different levels will depend upon the nature of the perceived challenge from the external environment (competitors, legislation, new technology, etc.) for that particular organization.

The training department as an agent for change

If training is fully integrated into the organization, the role of the training manager becomes much more wide-ranging—essentially that of an internal consultant on organizational change and development, as well as the more traditional role. Not all training managers are willing to take on this role for, as we shall see, the skills involved are very different to those traditionally associated with training.

Wellens (1979) discusses what he calls 'The broad view of training'. He argues that there is a basic difference in aims between the training function and that of personnel. The latter tends to see management as the administration of systems—formal procedures, agreements, rule books, keeping records, etc. Training is seen as the instrument for breaking new ground and bringing about change, whereas personnel is seen as a function for monitoring the *status quo* and a form of maintenance management.

There are two major problems in achieving the position which Wellens believes to be desirable for training. First, the range of skills available in the training department and, second, the development of a power base from which to implement organizational change.

Training started from a tradition of activities which helped individuals to perform identified tasks within jobs. Changing the focus from clearly specified jobs to the well-being of the organization implies a profound change in the skills required of the trainers. The skills of job analysis and in-class presentation of material, which are widely distributed in the population of trainers, become much less valuable than the problem-solving and political skills required for working successfully with line managers. These latter skills are not widely distributed among trainers. There is also the problem of the capacity of the training manager to make changes. He or she usually reports to the personnel manager and thus is often not in a powerful position to be pro-active in planning changes within the organization. Wellens argues for a manager of human resources who sits on the Board and who thus has the position necessary to be involved in forward planning. Not many companies have established such a post; perhaps that will change. In the literature, more co-ordinated and farsighted personnel policies are being widely recommended as being the key to improved company performance. The position of a manager of human resources would offer much greater opportunities for the co-ordination of personnel procedures, manpower development plans, recruiting and training and management development programmes.

Pettigrew, Jones and Reason (1982) reported a survey of the work of trainers within the chemical industry. The study began with an assumption that the training role was changing from the administration and conduct of training courses to one which involved more consulting and advising activities. What they actually found was that the patterns of role conception and behaviour varied across the sample and could be roughly divided into five types: the provider of training services, the passive provider, the training manager, change agents and those in transition from provider to change agent. The following definitions were used:

- The *provider* offers training services and systems which are primarily orientated to the maintenance and improvement of organizational performance rather than to changing the organization in any major ways. The role is fairly stable within the organization and has considerable legitimacy.
- The *passive provider* is more likely to sit back and wait for people to come for help. Many seem to be unaware of ways in which they might gain access to potential clients or build strategies for influencing key decision-makers in the organization.
- *Training managers* are mainly concerned with supervision of staff and the development and maintenance of the training function. They are often preoccupied with the need to develop a position of power by the use of written training policies or by links with senior managers.
- *Change agents* are concerned with organizational development and changing the culture of the organization. Those holding this role work on the basis of high personal acceptability as there is little legitimacy in the role *per se*.

The providers and passive providers were in the majority; less than one in ten of the trainers interviewed were classified as change agents.

Bennett and Leduchowicz (1983) identify four main types of role for trainers based upon two dimensions (see Figure 4.2). The horizontal dimension is one of orientation towards training as an educational process on the one hand, or as a process of intervention into organizational processes on the other. The vertical dimension represents an orientation towards maintaining the organization or changing it.

- *Caretakers* see the need for training to maintain the smooth running of the present systems and procedures within the organization, and adopt an educational approach. Courses are run off the job, are trainer-centred and highly structured.

Organizational
maintenance
orientation

CARETAKER   **EVANGELIST**

Traditional   Interventionist
educational   orientation
orientation

EDUCATOR   **INNOVATOR**

Organizational
change
orientation

Figure 4.2   *Types of role for trainers based on two dimensions*
Source: Bennett and Leduchowicz, 1983

- *Educators* see the need for training to change the systems, procedures or technologies in the organization, but also prefer to use traditional highly structured, educational, course-based approaches in order to achieve this.
- The *evangelist* sees training primarily as a means of maintaining the present systems and procedures but prefers to use a range of interventionist strategies. Most of these will be learner-centred and many will be based upon on-job assignments.
- *Innovators* adopt a range of interventionist strategies in order to change aspects of the organization. Quite often these strategies will include programmes for individual development and they will usually be interventionist in the workplace.

Bennett and Leduchowicz report that there is a strong tendency for trainers to want to move from the 'caretaker' to the 'innovator' role as the latter is frequently seen as an ideal type. Most trainers are, however, 'caretakers' and have themselves been trained by previous generations of 'caretakers'. The role is a comfortable one and there is considerable risk for them if they embark into uncharted territory. It is also the case that many organizations expect their trainers to design and deliver courses rather than bring about change.

The view of training which emerges from articles like those of Wellens, Pettigrew, Jones and Reason, and of Bennett and Leduchowicz can be summarized by contrasting what training departments have traditionally done and what they would be required to do if they were to function as agents of change:

- The *traditional/reactive* role involves training needs analysis at the job and individual level, then the development and running of courses. It is largely a role of responding to requests and it is a fairly stable function which is well understood by management.
- The *change agent/proactive* role involves individual and group counselling and working on group problems. It is largely a role of the catalyst and co-ordinator of management workshops and problem-

solving groups. Its primary focus is on developing human resources policy, particularly where this involves changing the culture. The role is complex politically and carries little legitimacy.

The implications of this second type of role are that the training manager must be more involved with policy-making and thus needs greater access to information. In order to carry out such a role successfully the training manager and the trainers who will be working in functions need to develop their boundary management, i.e.:

1 acquiring the resources to provide services
2 building relationships and promoting their image
3 protecting their integrity and position
4 co-ordinating activities with other roles and functions
5 exercising influence on key decision-makers

The trainers interviewed by Pettigrew, Jones and Reason (1982) used a number of power bases in order to attempt to manage these kinds of boundaries:

- *Managers* typically used a well-developed network of relationships, track record, positional power, policy documents, and top level political support. Crucial to the success of this role was the capacity to use knowledge of values and patterns of behaviour in the functional culture in order to influence that culture.
- *Change agents* and those in transition to that role typically used networks of relationships, track record, having access to information and the fact that they were perceived as being neutral.
- *Providers* used few power resources, mainly those of technical competence and political support from the immediate boss.

This work offers the beginning of a rationale for developing the role of the training department to include that of internal consultant on organizational change and development.

Further useful information may be found in the organizational change literature, where power bases for change agents are discussed. The most interesting approach is that by Pettigrew (1975). Pettigrew assumes that, because the various departments and functions will all compete for scarce organizational resources, it is useful to conceive of the organization as a political system. As change, particularly structural change, will have political implications for some groups within the organization, the success of any agent for change will be a consequence of his or her ability to mobilize power. Pettigrew discusses the situation confronting the internal consultant and argues that the ability to influence clients will be a function of the possession and tactical use of five power resources: expertise, control over information, political access and sensitivity, assessed status, and group support.

1 *Expertise*　In a sample of consultants, 55 per cent claimed that they had influence because they 'alone have the time and techniques to produce detailed and novel solutions to complex problems of planning' (Pettigrew, 1975, p 196). The implication here is that the consultant has singular possession of a valued area of technical competence which makes the client dependent.

2 *Control over information*   Burns and Stalker (1961) assert that information can become an instrument for advancing, attacking or defending
status. Pettigrew builds on this and argues that, as internal consultants
usually have contacts across departmental boundaries and with significant other organizations, they are well-positioned to take on the
role of gatekeeper. This offers them advantages with regard to access
to organizational communications and thus offers a source of power.

3 *Political access and sensitivity*   Political access is likely to be critical to
the acceptance and implementation of new ideas because the ideas
which succeed are likely to be those with the most powerful support.
The amount of support which an internal consultant achieves will be
a function of the structure and nature of formal and informal
interpersonal relationships. For political advantage, those who have
power in the organization should be included in these relationships.

4 *Assessed stature*   Consultants generally do not merely advise, they
persuade, negotiate and they exercise the power that they can mobilize.
An important constraint on this is the assessed stature of the consultant,
both in the centres of power and in immediate interpersonal relationships. The consultant's ability to demonstrate competence in previous
situations will contribute to this power base. When setting up new
consultancy relationships, assessed stature will often be influenced by
the ability to anticipate what is salient to the client. Pettigrew uses the
word 'salient' to refer not only to the client's specific expectations but
also to their more general interests such as political and careerwise.

5 *Group support*   A major constraint on political activity is the amount
of time and energy which it consumes. An important variable in this
is the amount and kind of group support given to the internal consultant by his or her colleagues.

Pettigrew sees the first three of these sources of power—expertise, control
over information, and political access and sensitivity—to be necessary
but not sufficient: 'Once he has the political access and understanding,
the consultant's ability to negotiate and persuade depends upon his
assessed stature with the appropriate figures in his political network'
(1975, p 205).

Many of these power bases could be used by training managers, but
whether they will gladly take on the challenge of the role of change
agent is difficult to say. It is more complex than the traditional one and
there is some doubt about whether most training departments have the
political skills necessary to be successful at it.

There is also the problem of knowledge of other disciplines like recruiting,
job evaluation and design, manpower planning and organizational
development. If we turn back to the discussion about trying to change
the interaction between people and the job situation in which they
found themselves (see Figure 1.2), it is clear that someone will need to
be thinking about structures, cultures, job design, reward systems and
selection. The training manager will often be unable to do this and the
implication seems to be that a team of specialists will need to be
involved in order to plan and carry through organizational changes. The
training department on its own will be unlikely to have all of the necessary
skills.

A further consideration is the organizational context in which many training departments find themselves. In some organizations change is not encouraged and management does not want a training department which is trying to operate as an agent for change.

Perhaps, at this stage, you might ask yourselves a few questions:

- Which of the five trainer types described by Pettigrew are present in your training department? Which is the predominant type?
- Which of the roles described by Bennett and Leduchowicz is most typical of your training department?
- What is the nature of the relationship between the line management and the trainers responsible for actually delivering programmes?
- How does the organization see the role of the training department? Does this coincide with the views of the trainers?

Summary

I started this part of the book with a statement that it is often worth while to evaluate a training programme by examining the processes by which it was designed and delivered. My basic premise is that the purpose of training is to improve the performance of individuals and thus increase the effectiveness of the organization. It follows that our first concern must be with the link between the training activities offered and aspects of organizational effectiveness. The first questions which should be posed are therefore:

- 'What changes are expected to result from this programme in terms of individual performance levels?'
- 'How are these changes linked to organizational effectiveness?'
- 'How do these changes relate to overall corporate objectives?'

When looking at the process of identifying needs, it is not sufficient only to look at the methods used; it is necessary to consider also the extent to which the three levels—organizational, job and individual—have been integrated.

If any particular training activity is to be an effective learning process, three elements should be present:

- The pre-programme preparation should be carried out to bring forward participants who are attending the right course for the right reasons
- The programme should be designed as a continuous set of activities structured to complement each other in facilitating learning
- Post-programme learning support is necessary to extend the training period and allow time for new methods of working to become established

If all these things are to happen, the status of the training department may need to be reviewed. This is, of course, a task for the organization as much as the training department, but the initiative may well have to come from the latter. Effective training implies a thorough understanding of the business plans and the organization's future objectives. Trainers will need to deal more directly with line managers and thus gain their trust and respect. This will usually result from a track record of actually helping to improve effectiveness. The business understanding of some trainers will also need to be developed as some of them will have to survive in the line by designing and implementing training programmes to improve performance.

PART TWO

Evaluating changes due to training

Introduction

In the first part of this book we looked at ways in which to evaluate the process of training. We emphasized that the process should be designed not only to achieve changes in the way the trainees think or the ways in which they act, but also that these changes should result in greater effectiveness in the workplace. We will now consider how to measure these changes. For the sake of clarity of presentation, we will focus on a specific aspect of change when considering methods of measurement— knowledge, skills, attitudes, etc. but actually the changes achieved will be multifaceted, with many different aspects integrated. Learning affects the whole person, and increases in knowledge or skills will usually result in different attitudes to some aspect of the work.

Organizational change occurs at many levels and takes many forms. Consequently, developing criteria by which changes can be evaluated may result in a range of indices. A good place to start is by establishing that learning has taken place at the individual level. This is one of the necessary conditions of those strategies of organizational change which focus upon people. It cannot be assumed, however, that individual changes will lead to a change in effectiveness and this will need to be evaluated in its own right.

We will first consider techniques intended to measure changes in individual levels of knowledge, skills and attitudes. Next, the criteria for evaluating increases in effectiveness at the individual, the team and the organizational levels will be discussed. Finally, we will outline some aspects of comparing the costs of training with outcomes.

5 Measuring changes in knowledge

Levels of knowledge

All jobs require the holder to have some knowledge. What type of knowledge is required? How can this be analysed? It is helpful, in attempting to answer these questions, to have some framework in which to carry out the analysis. One which has proved to be useful is to describe the sort of knowledge required at three levels:

1 The basic level is that of isolated pieces of information—ability to recall simple lists or state simple rules, knowing a range of simple facts about the job area. For instance, a counter-clerk at the Post Office would need to know what forms have to be filled in and what documents produced in order to apply for a vehicle licence disc.
2 A higher level is to be able to arrange a good many of the pieces of information into procedures, how to do things, how to order sets of actions. For instance, starting up a processing plant involves a series of actions which must be done in a certain sequence.
3 Higher still is the knowledge with which to analyse any particular situation for its key elements and thus to make a decision about whether procedure 'A' is more likely to be successful than, for example, procedure 'D'. This is essentially the skill to be able to select the most appropriate procedure or method of doing something, given the nature of the problem, the organizational context, etc. For instance, a social worker may have to decide whether a particular youngster's needs are best met by being left in the family of origin, or by being taken into care, either by fostering or in a residential home.

This is a hierarchical set and it is not possible to achieve the higher levels without knowledge at the lower levels. The function of training could, therefore, be seen as:

- analysing what is required at each of the three levels for satisfactory job performance
- discovering what the trainees know at each level before they attend the training
- trying to close that gap
- communicating to the supervisor or manager to what extent they are below satisfactory job performance levels at the end of training

The three levels of knowledge have quite different implications for the training process. Isolated pieces of information can be quite easily transferred by lectures to large groups or by paper-based texts or by programmed packages. All of these methods are relatively inexpensive. Procedures too can be learned fairly cheaply by using checklists and prompts plus, perhaps, some supervised practice.

The implications of the third (analytic) level are quite different. If this is to be achieved, the trainees will have to practise in realistic situations and make decisions about how to handle them. As this is actually a simulation of some aspects of the job, it will be much more expensive to design and it will take much more time to run than the work at the lower levels.

The implications for the sophistication of measurement of changes in knowledge are also different. It is relatively easy to test knowledge of isolated pieces of information and of procedures. This can be done by simple testing where the answers can easily be seen to be right or wrong. At the analytic level, the solutions to the problems posed will often have a qualitative aspect to them. This will imply that a subject expert will have to scrutinize the solutions and decide which are acceptable and which are not. With highly developed simulations, these decisions are built in but this is an extremely expensive process. For instance, flight simulators which allow the practice of a wide range of emergency procedures, cost airlines a minimum of £50 million.

Testing knowledge

Open-ended questions

The traditional way of testing knowledge in our educational system is by use of the essay. Questions like, 'Discuss the extent to which the Triple Entente contributed to the outbreak of the First World War' are said to distinguish between those who know some facts about this subject and those who do not. What such questions actually test is not so much what the student knows but how well he or she can assemble a logical argument on paper. This skill is important for success in many professions, including the jobs of lecturers who set such questions, but it is unimportant in many other jobs. This form of testing, when applied to training, is usually inappropriate, not because of the open-ended nature of the question, but because it is often testing a skill which is irrelevant.

Short answer items

Open-ended questions can be asked to test knowledge of isolated pieces of information and procedures. They can sometimes be used to test powers of analysis. The questions should start with a verb like:

State	Calculate	Describe (in your own words)
List	Determine	Write (short reports)
Label	Define	

The answer expected should be short and some indication of length should be specified.

It is relatively easy to write questions of this type in order to measure trainees' knowledge of a particular topic. The marking of the answers may, however, pose some problems. Some of these are listed here:

1 Answers may vary but still be correct.
2 It is difficult to mark them consistently as the decision criterion for correct/incorrect answers tends to drift over time.
3 A detailed marking guide is necessary.
4 The marking guide will often need some amendment after a few answers have been read in order to incorporate unforeseen alternatives.
5 Quite often people will disagree over whether a particular answer is correct. This implies that where there is more than one marker there will be problems of reliability.
6 It is necessary for the person marking the answers to be a subject expert and this may be an expensive use of such a person's time.

Objective test items

An alternative to testing by using open-ended questions is to ask the trainee to write one or two words, or to select the correct alternative from a number offered. With these objective test items the rules for scoring are made absolutely clear so that the answer can be recognized as being right or wrong and can be marked so by someone who knows nothing about the subject area being tested.

This kind of question is very suitable for testing low levels on our hierarchy but it takes some ingenuity to write them for higher levels. This has led to a folklore that objective test items are only suitable for very trivial scraps of knowledge. This is not necessarily the case. The Open University, for instance, does a lot of course assessment by using objective tests and some of the items are certainly not testing recognition of simple facts. An example is the sort of question where the understanding of a theory is being tested by asking which of a set of statements is consistent with the theory. Some of these questions are testing the ability to apply the theory in new situations, a procedure which is quite close to what we have called the 'analysis' level of knowledge.

Objective test items have the advantage over open-ended questions that they take less time to answer and the test can therefore cover a much wider area of the topic in the same time. They are also less likely to be testing the level of literacy of the candidates. They have the disadvantage of being much more difficult to write.

Multichoice questions

Multichoice questions consist of a stem and four or five alternative responses, and can be in the form of a statement or a question, for example:

Statement	Question
A tachometer indicates	What does a tachometer indicate?
a Road speed	a Road speed
b Oil pressure	b Oil pressure
c Engine speed	c Engine speed
d Battery charge	d Battery charge

The trainee circles or crosses the alternative selected; anyone with a marking brief can decide whether the answer is correct or not.

Simple guidelines are available for writing this kind of test item. Stems should:

- be clear and brief
- not include negatives
- not give clues by using key words which are repeated in the correct alternative answer

Incorrect alternatives (usually called distractors) should:

- all be plausible
- all be incorrect
- be arranged in a random order so that the correct answer cannot be guessed because of its place in the sequence of alternatives

General considerations are:

- each item should test a concept which it is important for the trainee to know
- no item should reveal the correct response to another item
- the items should be grouped by type so that the instructions can be made simple

True/false questions

Multichoice items are often difficult to write because sufficient plausible alternatives cannot be found. In this case, it is possible to use a specific form, the *true/false* item, for instance:

> '*Filet mignon* is obtained from best end of mutton'   True/False

With this type of item there is a greater likelihood that only trivial information will be tested. There is also the possibility of giving clues by using words like 'never' or 'always' in the stem as these are usually false statements.

Correcting for guesswork

It is clear that if a candidate is faced with a true/false test, knows nothing and guesses each item, he or she will score approximately 50 per cent. If it seems likely that some guesswork is taking place then a 'guessing correction' can be applied:

> True score = Number of items correct − Number of items wrong

With multichoice items there is less likelihood of guessing in a random fashion. If necessary, this likelihood can be reduced by requesting that the candidates should not guess but leave questions unanswered when they have no idea what the answer is. It is also possible to use a guessing correction with the formula now becoming:

$$\text{True score} = \text{Number correct} - \frac{\text{Number wrong}}{(\text{Number of alternatives} - 1)}$$

e.g. the candidate has 70 correct, 21 wrong and has not attempted 9 on a multichoice test with four alternatives:

$$\text{True score} = 70 - \frac{21}{(4 - 1)}$$

$$= 70 - 7$$

$$= 63$$

The amount of guesswork which is occurring is, in itself, an interesting measure of knowledge. People who have learned something do not need to guess unless the question is ambiguous.

Objective test items need some drafting skill as well as knowledge of the subject area and they need to undergo some pilot testing to ensure that the trainees do not find them ambiguous. Test items that have worked particularly well should be collected to form a test battery for future occasions. A way of refining them and selecting them for an item bank is described in the 'Item analysis' part of Appendix 1.

Test results contain a good deal of information which can be of use when evaluating training. The mean (or average) mark tells us how difficult the test was for the trainees. Comparison of two sets of scores from different groups of trainees will give an indication of whether one group learned more than the other. If test results are to be used for evaluative purposes (or for feedback), the test will need to be reliable, i.e. to consistently measure what it is supposed to be measuring. These issues of comparing sets of scores and establishing the reliability of a test are discussed in Appendix 1, 'Analysing test scores'.

Gain ratios   When we looked at a framework for analysing types of knowledge required, it was suggested that training could be considered as an attempt to close the gap between present and desired levels of knowledge. From this statement it would appear to be logical to measure knowledge before as well as after training and thus estimate the gain. There are problems in doing this. The most obvious is that it may be a waste of valuable training time to establish that the trainees know virtually nothing at the beginning of the programme. It is also necessary to produce two similar but different tests or the trainees will be alerted to the questions to be asked at the end of the programme and may concentrate on learning the answers to these particular questions rather than learning the principles which allow them to answer a range of similar questions.

There are some situations where it is worth while to pre-test as well as post-test knowledge. The gain ratio which can be calculated from this will give an estimate of the effectiveness of the programme. Using the formula:

$$\text{Gain ratio} = \frac{\text{Post-test score} - \text{Pre-test score}}{\text{Possible score} - \text{Pre-test score}} \times 100\%$$

a figure which takes values between 0 and 100 per cent will be obtained for each candidate. This represents how effective the programme was in teaching the particular individual what he or she needed to learn. The average gain ratio over a group of trainees gives a course effectiveness measure. As a guide one should expect an average gain ratio of about:

50 per cent with a good instructor and a good balance between
input and practice
70 per cent or better with individual instruction on programmed packages
20 per cent with short lectures followed by questions

These figures are empirical, based on studies of actual gains made, and
can probably be explained by the level of active learning involved in the
three methods.

Poor levels of gain may also indicate that the trainees do not comprise a
homogenous group. It is quite often the case that some know a good
deal about the topic before training and some know virtually nothing.
When this happens the tutors will pitch the learning rate at a level
which is too high for some and too low for others. If this is a serious
problem, it will be revealed because the gain ratios will tend to cluster
into two groups; high for people whose pre-scores were low, and low
for the others (or vice versa). The implication here is that a pre-test
could filter the candidates into two streams for more effective learning.

Pre-testing also sensitizes the trainees to those aspects of the programme which the tutors think to be important. This is widely used in
programmed packages as a way of motivating the learners by indicating
what the objectives are. Research on motivation has shown that many
adults appear to be trying to achieve goals which they have set themselves for much of their adult life (see, for example, Locke *et al.*, 1981).
This may be a source of energy which can assist in the training process.
Alerting trainees to the important aspects will also remove some of the
ambiguity and allow them to make more informed estimates of what the
programme might be able to offer them. What we are suggesting here is
that evaluation can be made an integral part of the process of learning
by utilizing the feedback on what is known and what needs to be
learned.

Following up knowledge-based programmes

Knowledge is actually taught in the belief that it is necessary for the job.
It follows that the evaluation of knowledge gain is often not complete
until the trainee has been followed back into the workplace to discover
to what extent the knowledge is useful. This is, essentially, to check that
the original analysis of what was required at each level is still an accurate
reflection of the reality. The initial investigation can be done by using
questionnaires but it may also be necessary to follow some of these up
by interviews. A suggested format for the questionnaire is given in Figure
5.1. (The design of questionnaires to collect data for particular purposes
is a skilled task. Some assistance with this is offered in Appendix 2,
'Designing questionnaires and analysing the data'.)

Where more than a third of respondents do not think that the knowledge is useful, or have not used it in the six months following training,
the relevance of the topic should be reviewed. This is best done by
interviewing a sample of people doing the job and their supervisors.
Where people say that they 'still have difficulty' they should be asked to
specify as far as they can the nature of the difficulty (there is space for

Topic (A detailed list of the areas covered on the programme)	How useful is knowledge of this for your job?			Have you used knowledge in this area since the the course?			Have you had any difficulty in applying this?		
	Very	Quite	Not	Often	Seldom	Never	No	At first	Still
Topic 1									
Topic 2									
etc									

Figure 5.1   *A questionnaire for following up knowledge-based programmes*

this printed on the back of the questionnaire form). It may be necessary, when these are examined, to seek further information about the precise nature of the difficulty. Again this is easiest to do during interviews. Information on designing interviews for evaluative purposes is given in Appendix 3.

A fourth area might be investigated on the front of the questionnaire by asking, against relevant topics, whether the reference material supplied was adequate. Sometimes if good written material is prepared for courses, the trainees can use this to help them after training and where this is possible the time spent on the topic during training can be reduced. It would certainly be worth asking them if this was the case. Off the job training is limited and expensive.

6 Measuring changes in levels of skills

Levels of skills

It is helpful to consider different levels of skills in a similar way to that which we used for knowledge. A suggested set of levels is given here:

1 The basic level with skills is to be able to communicate and for this it is necessary to be able to label items, to identify parts, to name the main assemblies of a machine, etc.
2 This level involves the ability to perform simple procedures, often with the use of instructions or notes. By simple procedures we mean actions like changing the wheel on a car, where there is a sequence to follow but each part of the procedure involves only a very simple skill.
3 This level is one of performing physically skilled actions. These usually involve hand–eye co-ordination and learning them requires considerable practice. Examples are planing a piece of timber to the required size, or typing at 70 words per minute.
4 Another level of skill is that involved in judging whether a piece of skilled work is of acceptable quality. For instance, deciding whether a piece of finished metalwork is satisfactory or not.

Once again, the length of time spent in training and the sophistication of the testing situation will increase with increasing levels.

Testing levels of skills

Skills should usually be tested with practical tests unless the skill of being able to do something can be assumed from the ability to state the correct sequence of actions. Listing the sequence is often a different skill, for instance, I can state how to strip, clean and assemble a carburettor, but when I do it the carburettor does not work properly afterwards.

Tests of skills fall into two main types:

- The trainee is set a task (for example, to repair an item) and the work is inspected at the end of the test period.
- The trainee is watched throughout the test so that the methods used can be assessed as well as the final product.

The first type of test is more economical in terms of the time spent by the tutors or testers. The second is more flexible as the trainee who makes an error in the initial stages can be put back onto the correct path by the tester and thus demonstrate ability to carry out other parts of the task. Some tasks will require the second type of test because the result will not show how well the work has been carried out. Some kinds of welding, for instance, need to be watched during the process as the quality of weld will not be obvious from a surface inspection.

Observation is a flexible technique for collecting evaluative data. It has some similarities with interviewing in that it can be quite unstructured or be supported by a very detailed schedule. Information about observing as an evaluative technique can be found in Appendix 4.

Serial	Sub-tasks	YES	NO
1	Stop on hard, level surface		
2	Apply handbrake	*	
3	Engage low gear	*	
4	Chocks or bricks in front and behind wheels	*	
5	Remove tools and spare wheel		
6	Check tyre pressure of spare and adjust if necessary		
7	Place jack under chassis nearest to wheel to be changed		
8	Loosen wheel nuts		
9	Jack up wheel approximately 1″ from ground		
10	Remove nuts—top nut last		
11	Remove wheel		
12	Place spare wheel on hub		
13	Secure top nut first	*	
14	Tighten all nuts, diagonally	*	
15	Lower jack—wheel on ground		
16	Tighten nuts fully	*	
17	Place spare wheel in carrier		
18	Clean tools		
19	Replace tools		
20	Question student on subsequent check (nuts to be checked at next inspection)		
	*These are critical tasks as they involve safety and, failure to observe them will result in a failure of the test.	Result PASS/FAIL	

Figure 6.1 *Changing a wheel: marking schedule*

Some written tests can also be practical tests. The 'in-tray' type of test which is often used in assessment centres is an example. The problems set are those likely to arise in the job, and the close relationship between the testing situation and reality of the job make it a very good predictor of job success. This is generally true of practical test as they can usually simulate job conditions much more accurately than tests of knowledge.

Practical tests have the disadvantage of being expensive because of the time required to supervise them and also because they often tie up expensive equipment. It is also more difficult to mark them reliably as the standards used will usually vary with different testers. Just how serious this is can be demonstrated by a simple exercise using electrical three-pin plugs. Six plugs are wired up to three core cables with one wired correctly and the others with defects, say:

a wired correctly	**d** wrong lead to earth
b live lead to neutral	**e** loose cable retainer bar
c too much bare wire	**f** one loose connection

A number of testers are asked to mark the finished work (given no information on standards or mark scales). Wiring such plugs is something that most people do regularly as most electrical equipment is sold without a plug. However, the standards which people find acceptable vary. On a number of occasions when we have used this exercise, we have found that some will accept plug C and/or E, some will even accept D. Most will mark out of 5 or 10 and a few will mark on a pass/ fail basis.

This emphasizes the general rule that detailed marking guides are necessary for practical tests. Also, that where more than one examiner is used, the marks should be compared and standardized on a few examples of work so that critical aspects of judgement can be agreed.

The same is true of performance tests. In this case it is often worth video recording a few attempts at the skill and asking the testers to develop a marking schedule. Figure 6.1 shows a simple schedule developed by this process.

Profiling skills

The use of the four levels of skill, and estimating at each level what adequate job performance means, allows the identification of individual needs for training. Effective training will also require some estimate of what the trainees are able to do before training. Often this can be assumed to be very little, but sometimes it is worth testing.

A large UK company which employs some hundreds of fitters to carry out servicing of central heating systems in homes was faced with the necessity of improving the quality of this service because of increasing competition. An off the job programme of three one-week modules was designed to cover the skills necessary to carry out the work. All the fitters were tested using fault finding exercises mounted on boards which represented the main types of heating system. The ways in which the fitters attempted these simple diagnostic tests were used to decide how many of the one-week modules each should attend. It was then possible to plan a programme of training courses which accurately met the skills needs across the population of fitters.

Profiling is widely used in education as a method of recording how far students have developed along a particular path. It can also be used in a training context for assessing where trainees are at present and where they should aim to be at the end of training. City and Guilds of London use a format of four attainment levels, each defined by a behavioural anchor, for example:

Using equipment	Can use equipment safely to perform a sequence of tasks after demonstration	Can select and use suitable equipment and materials for the job	Can set up and use equipment to produce work to standard	Can identify and remedy common faults in equipment
	20 May 90		◄ 30 June 90	

A discussion takes place between the trainee and the tutor. When the category which is thought to be most relevant is identified this box is dated. A second date is entered into one of the boxes to the right which is thus identified as the next objective and the date at which achievement of this will be reviewed.

This process of identifying bench-marks and then regularly checking progress against them could be widely used in skills training. The book by Rackham and Morgan (1977), which we mentioned when discussing ways of structuring learning events (p23), advocates the use of just such a process in the training of interpersonal skills.

The assessment centre has been used for many years as a method of selecting employees for promotion. The individuals being assessed are given a series of exercises which are thought typical of the work at the next level of seniority. For a typical management assessment centre there would be some evaluation of skills like communication, planning and organizing, analysis, judgement and delegation. There might also be some assessment of abilities like business sense or generation of creative ideas. Senior managers in the organization would be trained to use detailed observation categories and asked to do the assessment. The process can take anything from a half a day to three days.

More recently assessment centres have been used for the identification of development needs. The exercises are again based upon the analysis of what is required for success at the next level of seniority and the assessment is done in a similar way. The purpose is different as the areas which are identified as being weak are made the basis of individual development programmes.

The effectiveness of these programmes can be assessed by attendance at a second assessment centre after an interval of perhaps one year. The candidates are again assessed and improvements noted.

Another method of using the assessment centre as an evaluative tool was reported by Byham (1982). Managers who had completed four weeks of training in various management skills took a series of tests in an assessment centre together with a similar number who had not yet been trained. The two groups were matched for level in the organization, education and experience. The assessors were, of course, unaware of who had been trained and who had not. It was found that the group which had been trained performed better than the untrained group on all of the dimensions. They scored about 40 per cent better on skills like oral communication, problem analysis, judgement and delegation. They scored about 20 per cent better on dimensions like leadership and decisiveness.

Following up skills-based programmes

Technical skills which have been properly learned transfer easily to the workplace. The reason for following up skills training of this type is not so much to check on transfer as to ensure that the training time is being used effectively, i.e. to train for those skills which are actually required and to train people only to the level necessary.

The principal task is to check that the original needs analysis was correct. The questions which need answering include:

- Could they have easily learned the skill on the job?
- Do they do it often enough to make it worth while learning?
- Are the levels right or do they need further development on the job?
- Is that part of the job still done that way or are the trainers out of date?

Follow up questionnaires of the type in Figure 6.2 will provide a good deal of the information necessary. These should be sent to the participants some time after training when they have had some opportunity to experience the range of the job, usually between three months and a year depending upon the complexity of the work.

Tasks	How often			Is it difficult?*		
Since the course have you had to:	Never	Sometimes	Often	Never	At first	Still
Diagnose mechanical faults in . . .						
Repair or assist the repair of . . .						
Use . . .						
Supervise someone using . . .						
etc . . .						

* If it is still difficult please specify the reasons in the blank spaces on the back of this page.

Figure 6.2 *A follow up questionnaire for skills-based courses*

In the following up of skills training it will almost certainly be necessary to contact the supervisors and this can be done using a questionnaire. An example is offered in Figure 6.3.

Tasks	Is it necessary for him/her to do this?		Can he/she do it to your satisfaction?			Would you rather have trained him/ her to do this yourself?	
The trainee has been taught to:	Yes	No	Yes, without supervision	Yes, with supervision	No	Yes	No
Diagnose mechanical faults in . . .							
Repair or assist the repair of . . .							
Use . . .							
Supervise someone using . . .							
etc . . .							

Figure 6.3 *A follow up questionnaire for supervisors*

It is also useful to have an open-ended 'remarks' column on the right. Space can be made for this by printing the questions across rather than down a sheet of A4 paper.

It may be necessary to interview a sample of participants and their supervisors to discuss details of why things are difficult or why some performances are not up to standard. This might be done directly or by telephone. Sometimes supervisors want all ex-trainees to be able to do everything with a high degree of skill. It will rarely be possible or economic to train to that level off the job and a face to face discussion may be necessary to establish where the responsibility of the trainers finishes and that of the supervisor starts. Part of the responsibility for developing to operational standards must usually be taken by the supervisor, except in those rare situations where this is not possible (e.g. landing space capsules on the moon and then driving moon buggies).

7 Changes in attitudes and behaviour

Attitude change versus behaviour change

When we discussed how training programmes might be structured in order to increase the likelihood of their purpose, we emphasized the need to distinguish skills from attitudes (see p 20). In this section we want to consider this issue in more detail as the distinction is an important one. Indeed, failure to clarify the difference between skills training and attitude change can often result in confusion. This is not to suggest that the two are incompatible but rather that trainers need to decide which aspects of their programmes are addressed to skills and which to attitudes. In this way the process of evaluation can be designed to look at one aspect separately from the other and to give the appropriate feedback. Let us consider a working definition which will clarify this important distinction. An attitude is a tendency or a predisposition to behave in certain ways in particular situations, whereas a skill is an ability to perform a task well. Attitudes can be measured directly but are usually inferred from what people say or are seen to do. Changing someone's attitude to something may well change what they say or do but this will not *necessarily* follow. People behave in ways which they believe to be appropriate to the situation in which they find themselves so that other variables in the present situation may be more powerful in selecting behaviour than attitudes previously held.

The process of attitude training has four main stages:

1 Identify desirable attitudes which are expected to lead to some improvement, usually of culture or climate, in some part of the organization. The attitudes identified are usually of a fairly general nature like: positive management; consideration for subordinates; openness and trust in the workplace; being less prescriptive and more likely to delegate responsibility.
2 Assess where the participants are with respect to the desired attitude. This is usually done by self-analysis, often with an inventory. The participants' perceptions of their 'normal' work behaviour are classified and shown to have some categories which differ from the ideal.
3 Convince the participants of the value of the desired attitudes by giving examples, models or counselling. This is reinforced by allowing them to experience some success in experiential learning, perhaps by role plays.
4 If the training is done well, the participants accept the new attitude

and return to work. Here it is expected that they will display behaviour consistent with the new attitude.

As attitudes are measured or discussed early in the programme it is possible to reassess them towards the end and show changes in the expected direction. Often this is done in an informal way as an end-of-course discussion of 'what were the most important things for me?'. It is possible to make this more formal by developing action plans—'what will I do more of and what will I do less of when I return to work?'. There are also inventories which can be used early and late in the programme. Useful sources of these can be found in the book by Henerson, Morris and Fitzgibbon (1978) and also that by Cook *et al.*, (1981). The inventories will seldom be exactly what is required but the formats can be used to build up something specific for a particular programme.

Semantic differentials

A simple method of checking whether there has been a change of attitude, and in what direction, is to use a semantic differential of the type shown in Figure 7.1. The participants are asked to think about a particular concept, for instance, 'evaluation of training' or 'participative management', and to mark on each seven-point scale where their opinion lies. The opinions of the group are usually summarized by frequencies or averages to give some feel for what their overall attitude is to the concept.

The concept of participative management is:

Valuable	1	2	3	4	5	6	7	Worthless
Sincere	1	2	3	4	5	6	7	Insincere
Strong	1	2	3	4	5	6	7	Weak
Relaxed	1	2	3	4	5	6	7	Tense
Active	1	2	3	4	5	6	7	Passive
Warm	1	2	3	4	5	6	7	Cold
Fast	1	2	3	4	5	6	7	Slow

Figure 7.1 *A semantic differential*

The exercise is repeated near the end of the programme and any changes in attitude can be identified. The technique is neutral with respect to the direction of the changes. The trainers should be able to assess whether a change on any particular dimension is positive and this should, of course, be related to the objectives of the programme. It is also possible to measure whether the change is a significant one in the statistical sense, i.e. whether it is unlikely to have arisen by chance, by using a simple Chi-squared technique. Examples of how to do this can be found in Appendix 2.

Repertory grid

A more rigorous method of finding out what people's attitudes are towards a particular concept is to use a *repertory grid*. This technique asks the person whose attitudes are being investigated to consider a number of examples of the concept and to say what criteria he or she would use to distinguish between them. This is usually done during interviews but can be done in groups. For our purpose of evaluating change due to a programme, the group method will usually be more practical as a one hour interview with each individual separately is likely to involve too much time.

An example of the group method should help to clarify the procedure. Suppose we are about to start on a programme of interpersonal skills training with a group of junior managers. The starting point for the programme is to try to discover what are their concepts of good interpersonal skill. It should then be possible to develop a programme to start from this baseline and move the managers' views closer to those which are thought valuable within the organization.

Using a group rep-grid technique, each participant is asked to write down the names of six manager with whom they have worked: two who are thought to have very good interpersonal skills, two who are thought to be poor in this area, and two who are in-between. No attempt is made by the tutors to explain what they mean by interpersonal skills, as all the ideas must come from the participants. Each name is then written onto a small piece of paper, these are shuffled and then coded A, B, C, D, E and F.

They are now asked to draw out A, B and C from the six and think about what these three might do in work situations where interpersonal skills are involved. What is it that two of them might do that is similar? What is that one might do that the other two would probably not do? In this way they select a pair who are likely to behave in a similar way and a single who would behave quite differently from the three labelled A, B, and C. Each then writes down the pair description on the left of a prepared form as below.

Triad selection

Pair description	Triad selection						Single description
	A	B	C	D	E	F	
Supportive	*	*	*				Not supportive

Quite often these are opposite statements but this is not always the case.

Next they draw the papers labelled D, E and F from the six and repeat the process of deciding what two of them would do that makes their behaviour alike and what the other one would do that would be different. For instance:

Pair description	Selection						Single description
	A	B	C	D	E	F	
Listens to what I have to say				*	*	*	Pre-conceived ideas

It is important for the tutors to supervise this and to ensure that the descriptions which are being written down are about what managers *do* rather than personality traits. Quite often the trainees will want to write down things like, 'warm personality'. Statements like this are at too high a level of generality to help us decide what needs to be learned in order to demonstrate 'warmth'.

The procedure is repeated until they have written down a number of contrasts by comparing different combinations of managers. Drawing three from six in ten ways, for example, ABC, DEF, ACF, BDE, ADF, BEF, CDF, ABE, BCD, ACE, will ensure that each manager is entered into the comparisons six times and should give enough information on how each participant distinguishes between categories of interpersonal skill.

The contrasts so far are not related to judgements about what the participants think represents good practice. This can be elicited in interview but it is also possible to do it by a simple scoring process. On each line the participants score their contrasts on a one to six scale by giving the manager who is most like the pair description a score of 1 and the one who is most like the single description a score of 6. Then scores 2 and 5 are allocated to the next most like and so on with scores 3 and 4. For instance:

Pair description	A	B	C	D	E	F	Single description
Supportive	" 6	" 2	* 1	3	4	5	Not supportive
Listens to what I have to say	5	3	2	* 1	* 4	* 6	Pre-conceived ideas

Some will want to use shared rankings (equal 3, etc.) but they should not be allowed to do this.

When they have scored all ten contrasts, these scores can be correlated with their view of good interpersonal skills. This is done by each of them ranking the six managers who make up the A to F using 1 for best and 6 for worst at interpersonal skills. These numbers are written down on a separate piece of paper, say:

Overall effectiveness	A 6	B 3	C 2	D 1	E 4	F 5

The ranking on overall effectiveness is now correlated with that on each of the contrasts, for example:

Pair	A	B	C	D	E	F	Single
Supportive	6	2	1	3	4	5	Non-supportive
Overall	6	3	2	1	4	5	
Differences	0	1	1	2	0	0	= 4

Pair	A	B	C	D	E	F	Single
Listens	5	3	2	1	4	6	Pre-conceived
Overall	6	3	2	1	4	5	ideas
Differences	1	0	0	0	0	1	= 2

The differences in ranks are summed, regardless of sign, to give a score. The signs are ignored as it is the size of the difference which is important. Where the resulting score is small, i.e. 0 or 2, the description in the contrasts is defining what the participant means by good interpersonal skills. Because of the method of scoring, high scores will result when the *positive* description is on the right (i.e. the single description). Thus the highest possible scores (18 and 16) are also defining what the participant means by good interpersonal skills. (It is usually worth checking the arithmetic at this stage. There are six pairs and therefore all of the scores should be even numbers; those people who have odd numbers should recalculate the differences.) Contrasts which have scores of between 4 and 12 are ways in which managers differ, but are not closely related to the concept of good interpersonal skills. Contrasts which are not opposites will seldom correlate highly with the overall criterion. This is because they are not on a linear dimension which the theory of correlation requires. For our purposes this is not really a problem as we wish to use only those contrasts which are very close to the overall criterion.

The contrasts which have scored 0 or 2 or 16 or 18 can be examined with individuals to draw out what, for each of them, is the definition of good interpersonal skills. With a group these contrasts can be collected and displayed to give an introduction to the programme. One of our groups produced a list which included the following:

Gets the job done but with concern	—	Self-centred
Treats people as individuals	—	Stereotypes people
Encourages development	—	Discourages development
Adult reactions	—	Childish
Talks through problems with me	—	Unable to see my difficulties
Listens and then acts	—	Listens but does not do anything
Allows people to have discretion	—	Closely monitors

Some personality traits have slipped in here and these contrasts need further expansion. What was meant by 'adult reactions'? What behaviour would be classified as 'childish'? These are questions that would need to be asked. Discussing types of behaviour like this gave a good lead into talking about interpersonal skills and thus into the main topic for the week.

This group procedure takes approximately one and a half hours but it gives a good feel for the attitudes that the participants have towards the concept at the beginning of the programme. It also introduces the area as it requires them to think carefully about the subject and clarifies what they as individuals believe. Sometimes this actually confronts them with attitudes which they did not expect. A group of managers in the National Health Service who were attending a management course were asked to produce a set of contrasts which would distinguish between a good and a bad hospital patient. It did not surprise us, but it did them, to find that many produced a picture of a good patient as someone who would lie still and not complain.

Towards the end of the training the procedure above can be repeated and the results compared. As they will now be familiar with the process, the second attempt will take much less time—perhaps 45 minutes. Changes can be assessed in a number of ways:

- An improvement in the number of contrasts scoring 0 or 2 or 16 or 18. At the beginning most of them will have only a few such contrasts as their views about the concept are rather diffuse. At the end they should be much more focused on the area which has been discussed.
- There should be fewer personality traits and more descriptions of what people *do*.
- Many of the constructs being used should be close to those offered by the tutors, i.e. identifiable from the objectives of the programme.

The repertory grid is a sophisticated technique with many variations to suit particular situations. Other applications and some idea of its scope can be found in Stewart and Stewart (1981).

Following up attitude and behaviour change

It is possible to follow up changes in attitudes back to the workplace to discover to what extent they have been maintained, but it is doubtful if this will actually produce useful information. One is still left with the assumption that changes in attitude imply changes in behaviour at work. An approach which seems more likely to help with evaluation is through the use of behaviour scales to measure changes in the ways in which things are done.

Behaviour scales

The basic rationale of using behaviour scales is that they can make explicit what changes are expected to result from training and give some estimate of whether they are actually occurring.

We have already mentioned the pioneering work of Rackham and Morgan (1977) when we were discussing programme structures (p 23). The 13 categories of behaviour which they developed are shown in Figure 7.2. These categories are intended to provide a vocabulary for communicating frequencies of doing things and thus act as an aid to providing accurate feedback which the recipient can understand. Important categories are selected from critical incident studies of the kind of work to be learned.

The actual categories of behaviour used by Rackham and Morgan were developed over a number of attempts and eventually settled as:

Proposing behaviour which puts forward a new concept, suggestion or course of action (and is actionable).

Building behaviour which extends or develops a proposal which has been made by another person (and is actionable).

Supporting behaviour which involves a conscious and direct declaration of support or agreement with another person or concepts.

Disagreeing behaviour which involves a conscious, direct and reasoned declaration of difference of opinion, or criticism of another person's concepts.

Defending/attacking behaviour which attacks another person or defensively strengthens an individual's own position. Defending/attacking behaviours usually involve overt value judgements and often contain emotional overtones.

Blocking/difficulty stating behaviour which places a difficulty or block in the path of a proposal or concept without offering any alternative proposal and without offering a reasoned statement of disagreement. Blocking/difficulty stating behaviour therefore tends to be rather bald, e.g. 'It won't work,' or 'We couldn't possibly accept that'.

Open behaviour which exposes the individual who makes it to risk of ridicule or loss of status. This behaviour may be considered as the opposite of defending/attacking, including within this category admissions of mistakes or inadequacies provided that these are made in a non-defensive manner.

Testing understanding behaviour which seeks to establish whether or not an earlier contribution has been understood.

Summarizing behaviour which summarizes, or otherwise restates in a compact form, the content of previous discussions or considerations.

Seeking information behaviour which seeks facts, opinions or clarification from another individual or individuals.

Giving information behaviour which offers facts, opinions or clarification to other individuals.

Shutting out behaviour which excludes, or attempts to exclude, another group member (e.g. interrupting, talking over).

Bringing in behaviour which is a direct and positive attempt to involve another group member.

Figure 7.2 *Categories of behaviour*
Source: Rackham and Morgan, 1977, Fig 2.2, p 31

Thus, with appraisal interviewing the categories thought to be important to good performance might include a high rate of:

- seeking information—proposals, solutions to problems, etc.
- testing understanding
- summarizing
- supporting
- building

and a low rate of:

- proposing
- blocking/difficulty stating

The frequency with which the candidates show these behaviours in early practice interviews is fed back to them and discussed. They then have clear bench-marks against which to measure progress. The best place to do this behaviour tracking is, of course, in actual job situations, but it can also be used during off the job training.

Another, rather crude, way of doing this is to make explicit which parts of the annual appraisal categories will be likely to change as a result of the programme. Figure 7.3 offers an example taken from a course in 'Consulting skills'. The aspect of 'Interpersonal skills' has been extracted from the annual appraisal form and is used to communicate to the candidate and his or her employing manager which categories of behaviour are the target of the programme.

Interpersonal skills: Involves the establishing of sound, straightforward and fruitful relationships with people by having:

- the ability to look at a situation from the other
  person's point of view and balance it against   *Strong/Adequate/Weak*
  one's own perceptions
- *the ability to influence others*   *[S/A/W]*
- the ability to appreciate how another person
  feels—empathy   *[S/A/W]*
- the ability to handle conflict while maintaining
  a good relationship   *[S/A/W]*
- the ability to convey ideas and agreements with clarity   *[S/A/W]*

Figure 7.3 *A behaviour scale based on an appraisal form*

During the programme the participant keeps a log of perceived improvements in these areas, and this is a tracking of attitude change as much as anything. The format also gives a clear rationale for the employing manager to make pre- and post-training comparisons in terms which are well understood within the company. It can thus be used in evaluating behaviour change at work.

It is also possible to take the objectives of the programme and translate them into statements of what people are more likely to do after the programme. Two examples are given in Figure 7.4, one from a programme on 'Positive management' and the other about 'Consideration' as part of a management course.

The rationale is again that of making explicit what changes in behaviour are expected and the format can be used before and after by the candidates themselves and by their managers to give estimates of attitude and behaviour changes.

Positive management	Never 0–19	Seldom 20–39	Sometimes 40–59	Generally 60–79	Always 80–100%
1 Thinks ahead and develops plans rather than constantly clearing up problems	☐	☐	☐	☐	☐
2 Thinks in terms of objectives rather than vague generalizations and makes them both clear and realistic	☐	☐	☐	☐	☐
3 Takes decisions rather than procrastinating or passing problems up to the next level	☐	☐	☐	☐	☐
4 Co-ordinates the group's activities and checks on progress to achieve objectives	☐	☐	☐	☐	☐
5 Deals with sub-ordinates as individuals and makes each accountable for a specific set of responsibilities	☐	☐	☐	☐	☐

etc. (The scale will need to be at least ten items long to give good reliability)

or **Consideration**	Never	Seldom	Sometimes	Generally	Always
1 Welcomes new ideas and alternatives	☐	☐	☐	☐	☐
2 Gets the approval of subordinates on important matters before going ahead	☐	☐	☐	☐	☐
3 Expresses appreciation personally to people who do a good job	☐	☐	☐	☐	☐
4 Makes opportunities to develop people as individuals	☐	☐	☐	☐	☐
5 Knows when individuals have problems, is helpful and supportive	☐	☐	☐	☐	☐

etc. (again, at least ten items)
Organizational constraints might make it impossible, but the people best qualified to give this sort of information are subordinates!

Figure 7.4 *Scales for changes in behaviour*

8 Changes in levels of effectiveness

The ultimate objective of training and development is to increase effectiveness in part of the organization. This is why the organization invests money in it. Yet many will argue that training, and in particular management training, cannot be evaluated against organizational effectiveness. This is either because the changes due to training become indistinguishable from the effects of other events or because the effort of an individual has little effect upon the performance of the organization as a whole. There is some truth in these arguments. It is difficult to isolate the effects of training from other factors and it may be impossible to do this if the criteria by which change is to be monitored have not been established before the training is designed. It is also true that the efforts of any one individual are unlikely to have a noticeable effect on the balance sheet at the end of the year.

There is, however, no need to use such a general criterion when looking for improvements in organizational effectiveness. It is possible to focus on a small part of the organization and to link improvements in its performance with training interventions. In this section we will show how this can be done. Where possible we will use actual cases to support the argument.

Individual changes in effectiveness

Most training and development activities focus on the individual with the intention that the learning will enable him or her to become more effective either in the present job or one which is shortly to be attempted.

If the training need which is to be met is identified in terms of the improved performance which should result (rather than that 'Mr X needs to attend course Y'), then it should be possible after the programme to assess whether this improvement has taken place. This may be quantifiable as an increase in productivity. It might also be expressed as having a wider range of skills and thus offering increased flexibility of employment.

In an earlier section on using behaviour scales for assessing change (p 59), it was suggested that these could make explicit what changes were likely and that it might be possible to integrate them with annual performance appraisal categories. If this can be done, the employing managers will be able to provide evidence of whether changes have taken place and, if so, whether increased effectiveness is the result. The study by

Latham and Saari (1979) was referred to (p 22) when we were discussing behaviour modelling as a training method. One of the methods of assessing increased performance in this study was an improvement in ratings on the annual appraisal. It was also possible to show increased productivity in the sections for which the supervisors were responsible.

One way of facilitating the transfer of learning back to work is by the use of action planning during training. At intervals during the training, for instance, daily on a five-day course, the participants are asked to focus on the utility of what has been discussed. This can be done by giving out coloured sheets of paper and asking each participant to write down two or three things which have been covered during the day which are thought likely to be particularly useful back at work. They should also make a short note against each on how they intend to make use of it. Some sharing and discussing of these will give useful feedback on what they think is important learning, but the main purpose is to focus on utility and build up an action plan for when they return to work. Towards the end of the programme they cluster the items from the sheets into areas and then arrange them in some order of priority. The action plan for, let us say, the next six months is now drafted by putting some time frame on each area to be tackled. It will also be necessary to write down against each area likely countervailing forces and how these are to be overcome. The questions which need to be addressed will include the following:

- Will this action have an effect on other people? How will they react to it?
- Whose authority will be necessary to implement this action? How do I ensure that this will be available?
- What organizational constraints are likely to prevent this action? What can be done to ease them?

The action plan is a piece of positive management. It forms a set of goals to be achieved and gives a time frame and rationale for each of them. It can be lodged with the course tutors and followed up later. Whether or not this happens, the plan should be discussed with the employing manager before or after return to work. During the follow-up some six months later, questions like the following can be asked:

- How much of your action plan have you been able to implement?
- Which actions have been shelved and why?
- What positive benefits in terms of effectiveness in your part of the organization have resulted from carrying out your action plan?

A specific form of action planning is through the use of an organizational project as the focus for the learning, with input from tutors at stages throughout the project. This project often has as a focus the increased effectiveness of a part of the company, and can show a good return for the investment in training. An example of this was described by Woodward (1975). The programme investigated was for supervisors and led to a National Examinations Board in Supervisory Studies qualification. There was formal coursework, mainly on theories of management, which was examined. There was also a work-based project which was intended to show the advantages of good supervisory practice. Woodward was unable to show any differences in ways of working as a result of the theoretical part of the course.

This ought not to surprise us. We have considered good examples of the processes which are needed in order to change the ways in which people do things at work. Theoretical input on the nature of management, without role play or work-based practice, is not one of them. Woodward was able to estimate the benefits of the project work. Six of the 12 showed positive benefits. Averaged over the 12, the return on training investment (course fee, travel, subsistence, equipment costs, pay of trainees and covering costs) was 2.9 : 1.

In the Department of Occupational Psychology at Birkbeck College, University of London, we have been encouraging our PhD students to form into groups (cohorts) in order to participate in mutual exchange of ideas, experience and learning (action learning sets). For example, a topic in which one of the lecturers is interested (e.g. stress at work, organizational change in the public section, evaluation of training) is selected as the theme. A cohort of four to six students who are interested in the topic is selected from applicants and each carries out his or her own *work-based* research. The main theme of the research is negotiated with the organization to which the student belongs and a senior manager takes responsibility for facilitating access. The group meets at least once a month to discuss plans and progress. Most of the meetings are devoted to discussing, in some depth, issues raised by one of the cohort. The main focus here is to develop the ability of each student to carry out research and thus to reach Doctoral standard. The process is more successful than the more normal one of individually based PhD programmes (which are also run concurrently) probably because it offers a good deal of support and encouragement to part-time students who otherwise become quite isolated for long period. The work-based projects are often valuable to the organization and show a good return on investment (academic fees for three years plus some two dozen days away from work discussing work-related issues).

Changes in the effectiveness of teams

Introduction

Team development is intended to improve the effectiveness of a group of people whose jobs require that they work together. It assumes:

- that the group has some reason for existing, some common goals and problems
- that interdependent action is required to achieve the goals or solve the problems
- that it is valuable to spend time in trying to understand and improve the way in which group members work together to achieve their tasks

Team development activities may focus on working relationships or on action planning. There are three main models: problem-solving, interpersonal, and role-identification.

- The *problem-solving* model encourages the group to identify problem areas which are affecting the achievement of group goals. Action planning is then used as a method of tackling the problems.
- The *interpersonal* model attempts to improve decision-making and problem-solving by increasing communication and co-operation on the assumption that improving interpersonal skills increases the effectiveness of the team.
- The *role-identification* model attempts to increase effectiveness by increasing understanding of the interacting roles within the group.

It is, of course, possible to combine the different models. For instance, the Blake and Mouton (1964) Managerial Grid is a combination of problem-solving and interpersonal approaches. For simplicity we will select a well-known example of each of the three models separately and examine the problems of trying to use them to improve the effectiveness of teams.

Problem-solving groups

The most widely used example of the problem-solving model is found in 'quality circles'. A quality circle is a small group of people involved in similar working situations who meet to discuss work-related problems. They usually volunteer to do this, i.e. it is not part of their job description. Implicit in the definition of a quality circle is that it is sanctioned by the organization and meets in the firm's time. The group:

- brainstorms problems
- agrees priorities
- selects and defines the problems to be tackled
- works together to collect data, etc.
- agrees possible solutions to problems
- presents proposals to management

The group has a leader who may be the supervisor, but the group sometimes elects its own leader from among the members. At least in the early stages, the group will also have a facilitator who helps with process issues.

The concept of quality circles was developed by the Japanese during the 1960s to introduce worker participation into quality control activities. It is estimated that there are now about one million circles in Japan. Noting increasing evidence of Japan's effectiveness in manufacturing, many western management specialists visited Japan to attempt to discover 'the secret'. They often came back with the view that the quality circles were largely responsible for the increasing competitiveness of Japanese products.

Hayes (1981) disputes this. He argues that Japanese firms are well-managed and they have well-trained workforces. Both the workforce and management continually strive for perfect products and error-free operations. Hayes argues that, given these factors, manufacturing success is inevitable and the quality circles are a reflection of the company cultures rather than a cause of their success.

Quality circles have become popular in the UK and the USA. Inevitably, however, some things have changed in translation from the Japanese. In particular, western quality circles seem not to be so obsessed with quality control; they are often used as a way to increase worker participation. Robson (1982), for instance, gives the impression that here, at last, is the way to get management of the Theory Y-type into organizations. (McGregor's Theory Y (1960), if you remember, assumes that the workforce will want to exercise self-direction and will seek responsibility.)

In order for quality circles to flourish Ishikawa (1968) has identified eight main principles:

1 All levels of senior management must agree to support, encourage and listen to* circle activities.
2 Management must not use circles to further their own pet ideas. Circles must be free* to pursue their own priorities.
3 Management must be patient*—circles do not produce change over-night.
4 Managers must be prepared to accept failures* without recrimination but with encouragement.
5 Participation must be present in every step of the process.
6 Circle leaders and facilitators must be carefully chosen, well-trained and credible.
7 Facilitators must be given enough time* and support for them to carry out their activities of improving group processes.
8 Circle membership must be voluntary*.

Those items which are marked * are aspects of organizational culture which are often lacking in western organizations. The Ishikawa principles, which are extracted from the Japanese experience, predict with remarkable accuracy the failure of quality circle programmes in the UK and the USA. Violation of one or more of these principles usually leads to the failure of the quality circle.

Dale and Ball (1983) carried out a survey of 86 companies in the UK which were supporting over 1000 quality circles. For our purpose the main interest is in criteria of success.

Some 92 per cent of the companies claimed that their quality circles programme was successful. The main reasons given for this were, for example, thorough consultation at all levels in the company and full management commitment to the concept. Also thought to be important was a controlled and gradual development without expectation of immediate cost savings. Thorough training and the selection of an enthusiastic facilitator were also considered to be essential.

Members of the circles found that there were benefits: increased job satisfaction, better teamwork within the department, recognition of their achievements and better relationships with members of management were quoted.

There were also benefits to management and the three considered most important were that first-line supervisors were placed in a leadership role, that many problems were solved at grass roots level thus allowing management to concentrate on higher priority items, and that it was possible to identify future managers among the quality circle membership.

Overall the companies felt that the main benefits derived from the investment in quality circles were:

- increased involvement of employees
- improvement in quality and productivity
- a reduction of the barriers between management and shopfloor
- improvement in communications across the company

Dale and Ball conclude that quality circles may lead to significant cost savings, but in some organizations they will do no more than make minor improvements. However, quality circles often improve the quality of working life and this is a worthwhile gain.

There is, of course, the other side of the coin—some quality circle projects fail. Dale and Hayward (1984) discuss some of the reasons for these failures. Most of these, as we stated above, could be attributed to disregarding one or more of the principles extracted by Ishikawa.

Working on interpersonal skills

Where team development is undertaken using an interpersonal model, the intention is to increase communication, sharing, trust, collaboration and cohesiveness within the group. This was, of course, the intention of the T-Groups which were so popular in some American organizations in the 1960s. The T-Group has had a bad press in evaluation literature, usually because individuals were required to attend and deeply resented the intrusion to their privacy which was involved. More recent forms of team development are rather less intrusive and there is less coercion to attend.

In deciding whether team building is appropriate in the first place, Weisbord (1985) suggests that the senior manager should call a meeting to introduce the idea of team development, state the management goals and request further discussion on the matter. If a consultant is hired or the organization has an experienced team builder, the team members would next hold a meeting with him or her to decide whether or not to go ahead. Often the team builder will interview members to identify their concerns, their objectives, the problems each faces, and the type and degree of help which they need from each other. This process can be aided by surveys or questionnaires which diagnose teamwork problems. Once the team builder has collected this data, he or she feeds it back to the team in summarized form and invites discussion on the setting of priorities. Team members will also be asked to explore the costs and benefits of continuing the process and, if the decision is made to proceed, a schedule is negotiated and drawn up.

One of the most accessible programmes designed for team development using the interpersonal model is that by Woodcock (1979). Types of teamwork problems are identified by using a questionnaire and they are grouped under the following headings:

- Clear objectives and agreed goals
- Openness and confrontation

- Support and trust
- Co-operation and conflict
- Sound working and decision-making procedures
- Appropriate leadership
- Regular review
- Individual development
- Sound intergroup relations

The questionnaire highlights problem areas by frequency of mention and this suggests priorities for team building. In the manual there is a short lecture on each teamwork problem and developmental activities are offered which, it is hoped, will allow the group to work through the problem area.

Woodcock argues that team building should take the group through four stages:

1 The *underdeveloped* group where most people concentrate on their own problems and are not much interested in those of others
2 The *experimenting* group where 'risky' issues can be aired
3 The *consolidating* group where consensus is achieved by working on interpersonal process issues
4 The *mature* group where the emotional needs of all are met

The question which must be raised, and which Woodcock ignores, is whether this shift from 1 to 4 is necessary for all groups in order for them to work together effectively. Critchley and Casey (1984) discuss when team building is appropriate and when it appears not to be. They see team building as being most useful when the group has to make decisions which involve a great deal of uncertainty. Here input is needed from every member of the group and all available expertise, experience and creative ability needs to be drawn upon. If this is to happen, the group will need to have high levels of trust and openness, and this will imply that feelings are part of the work situation and need to be dealt with. Top management groups dealing with strategic problems personify the type of group which needs team development. In many management teams the work situation is rather more routine than this, does not include high levels of uncertainty and there is not the necessity to share all the information available. With these groups, team development is not indicated and, as it is likely to surface interpersonal problems between members of the group, it may be counter-productive.

Critchley and Casey offer a model which helps in the decision of when team building may be appropriate and which we have adapted and show as Figure 8.1

The distinction is made between 'puzzles' (the answer exists some-where—just find it) and 'problems' (no answer is known to exist). Most work groups are said to be working at the puzzle level almost all of the time and for these groups 'it is absurd to indulge in work with people's feelings' (1984, p171) as this will raise unnecessary interpersonal difficulties without helping the work. The main requirement for most groups is that they have interpersonal skills like co-operation, communi-

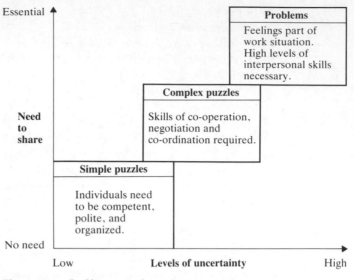

Figure 8.1 *Problems, puzzles and team processes*
Source: adapted from Critchley and Casey, 1984

cation, listening and negotiating so that they have, when necessary, the skills to solve complex puzzles.

Weisbord (1985) sees a further use for team building as an effective preparation for change in that it opens up lines of communication and creates the active involvement which is necessary to overcome resistance to change in a constructive way.

In an extensive and critical review of the role of team development in organizational effectiveness, Woodman and Sherwood (1980) report that team development based upon interpersonal skills is often used as an aid to the formation of a new team, but their main conclusion is that the available research does not provide a conclusive link between this kind of team building and improved work group performance. What does seem likely is that these team development activities have some effect on attitudes—how one feels about others, the workplace, the value of the team, satisfaction with the work. Many would argue that improvement in indices of these attitudes would be valuable in themselves and would be likely to be closely associated with other performance measures.

Identification of roles

The role–identification model approach treats the group as a set of interacting roles and attempts to increase effectiveness by a better understanding and allocation of these roles. Each member of a team is considered to contribute in two ways: (1) in a functional role, drawing on professional and technical knowledge and (2) in a team role, helping the progress of the team towards achieving its objectives. This implies that a team can only deploy its technical resources to best advantage when team members recognize and use their team strengths. Observation of groups where three or four people who are outstanding in their field are recruited to form a team, indicates that the team performs in a disappointing way—usually everyone produces ideas and no-one develops them.

One of the best known team role approaches is that advocated by Belbin (1981). Eight team roles are described:

1 Someone with leadership capabilities: calm, assertive, welcomes ideas, self-confident—*the chairperson*.
2 An ideas person: intelligent, creative and serious—*the plant*.
3 Someone to evaluate suggestions: intelligent, analytical, practical and tough-minded—*the monitor evaluator*.
4 Someone who carries out agreed plans in a systematic manner: practical, hardworking, predictable—*the company worker*.
5 Someone to keep a sense of urgency within the team: anxious, conscientious, a tendency to worry—*the completer–finisher*.
6 Someone to explore and report on ideas from outside the group: enthusiastic and extroverted—*the resource investigator*.
7 Someone who challenges ineffectiveness, who directs attention to the setting of objectives and priorities: dynamic and highly strung—*the shaper*.
8 A team builder who fosters team spirit and improves communication between the members: socially aware, sensitive—*the team worker*.

It is not necessary to have eight people in the group, however, someone aware of and capable of carrying out each of these roles should be present. If there is not a good match between the attributes of the team members and their responsibilities (for instance, if the chairperson is actually an ideas person) then the team will not perform effectively.

You might like to consider combinations of these roles and think about what impact they might have on the effectiveness of a group. What is the likely effect of having:

• A chairperson who is a teamworker?
• A chairperson who is a shaper?
• Two or more shapers in the group?
• No company workers or completer–finishers?
• No one in the resource investigator role?

In a consultant's role Belbin would test members of a group to discover which characteristics they have and what roles they should play.

• Intelligence is tested using the Watson–Glaser Critical Thinking Test. This indicates how people use their intelligence to evaluate arguments, draw inferences, make deductions, etc.
• Personality is assessed using the Cattell 16 PF questionnaire.
• Personal preference is assessed by using a projective test. The candidate is given a form on which 100 paired names are printed, e.g.:

Ian Botham	David Gower
Humphrey Bogart	James Cagney
Navratilova	Evert

Each member of the group ticks off which of each pair is preferred and then writes a word beside the name indicating the quality which justifies the preference. These qualities are categorized—talent, achievement, personality, etc.—and the dominant pattern is said to give main constructs for judging people and therefore to indicate the type with whom he or she could work well.

As well as the theory behind the definitions, Belbin (1981) offers a self-perception inventory which helps people to identify the roles in which they think that they are strongest so that they can make a better contribution to the group by trying to fill these roles. If each member of the team completes and scores this inventory, it is possible to use the information to examine whether the group has strengths in all of the roles. It is also possible to see where role conflicts are likely to occur. Encouraging people to develop roles in which they think that they have strengths, but which they are not currently filling, is a plausible way to improve the quality of the teamwork. It seems likely that with an existing group, peer ratings can reveal most of the characteristics which are of interest. It would be very interesting to investigate the differences between self-perceptions and the group's perceptions of behaviour within the group, although there are problems in doing this. For instance, many people are not very perceptive about their own abilities and skills, and it is also the case that some of the roles are more highly valued than others in social terms. It is quite likely that the group will need a facilitator who is not one of its members if it is to resolve these problems.

Belbin's theory is based upon research using management games where team effectiveness was measured in terms of 'financial' results. This is an interesting training and evaluation procedure—to form teams through a role analysis and then test their performance in the controlled situation produced by a management game. There is, however, a question concerning the validity of this as there is not much evidence so far that the identification of roles results in increased performance in job settings. The model may well have some value in setting up project teams where roles can be allocated and the strengths of others (apart from their technical ability) need to be understood. It probably has greater value in providing a vehicle for helping the group members to conceptualize the roles necessary and for developing their skills in roles which they had not previously considered. It ought to be possible to evaluate on a pre-/post-basis how peoples' perceptions of their roles have changed and the extent to which they perceive the group as being more effective as a result of training. Such information has not yet been published.

Evaluation of team-based strategies

Not much of the published research on various strategies for team building permits unambiguous interpretation of the results (Woodman and Sherwood, 1980). The main problem is one of internal validity, i.e. the confidence with which conclusions can be drawn from a set of data. The research designs are usually poor and it is not possible to rule out alternative explanations for the effects which are reported.

The problem-solving approach is easier to evaluate than the others as the problems to be tackled are clearly identified and defined and they often have an obvious connection with some measure of organizational effectiveness. It can often be argued that the increase in effectiveness would not have occurred without the development of the team.

The interpersonal approach is usually evaluated in terms of perceived effectiveness. This is not very convincing if the intervention needs to be justified in terms of organizational benefit, since the results are likely to be measured as changes of attitude rather than of behaviour. There is also the problem of internal validity as, without the use of control groups, it may be difficult to rule out factors other than the team development process which could have affected the attitudes measured.

Evaluation is even more difficult with the use of the role clarification approach in an organizational setting. The composition of each group is unique and the assessment of its improved effectiveness will therefore have the format of a case study. It should be possible to analyse a set of these to indicate perceived improvements in group working which support the theory. These perceived improvements will certainly imply increased awareness on the part of the group members, but the links with improved effectiveness of the organization are not easy to predict.

Changes in organizational effectiveness

Introduction

Organizational effectiveness is not a simple concept with the balance sheet at the end of the year as the only criterion to be assessed. There are many ways in which one can look at it, and many writers have offered sets of criteria. One of the early attempts was that of Georgopolous and Tannenbaum (1957) who evaluated effectiveness in terms of productivity, flexibility and the absence of organizational strain. More familiar is the approach of Blake and Mouton (1964) which seeks the simultaneous achievement of high production-centred and high people-centred methods of management. Katz and Khan (1978) argue for growth, survival and control over the environment.

A more recent classification has been offered by Cameron (1980) who considers that almost all views on organizational effectiveness can be summarized under four headings:

1 *Goal-directed* definitions focus on the output of the organization and how close it comes to meeting its goals
2 *Resource-acquiring* definitions judge effectiveness by the extent to which the organization acquires much needed resources from its external environment
3 *Constituencies* are groups of individuals who have some stake in the organization—resource providers, customers, etc.—and effectiveness is judged in terms of how well the organization responds to the demands and expectations of these groups
4 *Internal process* definitions focus attention on flows of information, absence of strain, and levels of trust as measures of effectiveness

We have found this classification of Cameron's to be very useful when discussing evaluation of training events with line managers. It is possible to consider effectiveness at levels lower than that of the whole organization and thus to build up a matrix like that in Figure 8.2.

The matrix can be used to discuss desirable changes in effectiveness

	Individual (my work)	Work Group (my section)	Function (my dept)	Regional level	Organiza-tional level
Goal-directed					
Resource-acquiring					
Satisfying constituencies					
Internal processes					

Figure 8.2 *The organizational effectiveness matrix*

which might accrue from training or development events. These should be identified by type of effectiveness and the level at which they will be measured. First of all, it is important to establish what criteria the line managers are actually using to assess effectiveness and by what criteria they themselves are being judged. In order to explain how this might be done, we need a more detailed description of the types.

Goal-directed   The most widely used approach to effectiveness focuses on meeting goals and targets. Directing and sustaining goal-directed effort by employees is a continuous task for most managers, but assessments will usually be a series of point measures over time. Most organizations use basic measurement of work output to meet *product* goals, where the emphasis is on quality or quantity, variety uniqueness or innovativeness of whatever is being produced. Types of indices which are usually available are:

Quantity	**Quality**	**Variety**
units produced	defects/failure rate	diversity of product range
tasks completed	reject rates	rationalization of product range
applications, etc. processed	error rates	
backlogs	rework	
turnover	scrap	
units sold	waste	
money collected	shortages	
on-time deliveries	accidents	

There are also *system* goals which emphasize growth, profits, modes of functioning, return on investment, etc. Criteria which might be available are:

---

productivity	rates of achieving deadlines	work stoppages
processing time	output per person/hour	supervisory time
profit	on-time shipments	amount of overtime
operating costs	percentage of quota achieved	lost time
running costs	percentage of tasks incorrectly done	machine down-time
performance/cost ratio	efficiency	frequency of accidents
length of time to train new employees		accident costs

Increases in manpower, facilities, assets, sales, etc., compared with own past state and with competitors.

Most of the techniques which are used for monitoring the achievement of system goals are fragmentary because they focus on a specific part of the company. Some method of looking at the workflow through the organization, perhaps like that described by Chapple and Sayles (1961), can overcome this problem and offer criteria by which system goals can be assessed at the level of the whole organization.

Following a major rethink on the direction of its 'Regular Service' business, the East Midlands Region of British Gas decided to shift the emphasis away from large contracts and towards an increase in the smaller domestic work. In order to make this new policy work 'Business development' days were run for higher and middle managers, selling skills courses were introduced for telephone staff, and 'Improving present performance' workshops were run for both engineering and administration staff.

A key feature of all the training was that line managers played a central role with professional trainers acting as facilitators.

Clear targets were set for the programme—an increase in the level of penetration into the domestic regular service market by 30 per cent and tripling of the revenue from all categories of Regular Service contracts. In fact the contract values more than tripled between 1986/7 and 1987/8 and market penetration also improved markedly. A bonus was the way in which the organization benefited from the commitment to teams which the success of this project brought.

Source: National Training Awards 1988, The Training Agency

Acquiring resources

Looking at resources changes the emphasis from outputs, goals and targets, to inputs designed to achieve some competitive advantage. At the level of the organization, the evaluation can be a comparison with major competitors, or against 'how we did last year', or against some ideal desired state. At lower levels, increased flexibility is often the measure which is used. Criteria which might be available for assessing increases in effectiveness include:

increases in number of customers	increase in the pool of trained staff
new branches opened	skills for future job requirements developed
new markets entered	
takeover of other organizations	increased flexibility in job deployment developed
ability to change standard operating procedures when necessary	readiness to perform some task if asked to do so

Devolving accountability and responsibility to departments is widely seen as contributing to the flexibility of organizations faced with an ever changing environment. Training is a necessary part of this process and can be evaluated on the basis of what effects would have been likely if no training had been offered.

Early in 1986 it was realized that the internal maintenance engineering costs at the Tees and Hartlepool Port Authority docks were excessive in relation to the volume of cargo throughput. One way of cutting costs was to improve the effectiveness of the craftsmen by training them in other skills in order to achieve multiskill flexibility. Following negotiations with the trades unions, it was agreed that each of the six 'maintenance' crafts would be trained in specific additional skills (for example, boilermakers would also do automotive mechanics and electrics).

In the twelve months subsequent to the training the throughput at the two docks increased by 24 per cent without any increase in the maintenance workforce and total profits rose by 32 per cent. Job satisfaction and morale have risen and a pattern of more productive work practices has been established for the future.

Source: National Training Awards 1988, The Training Agency

Constituencies

Effectiveness can be judged by the extent to which the organization meets the expectations of groups whose co-operation is important. Assessment of effectiveness will be against criteria like the following:

customer complaints	company image surveys
returned material	customer relations surveys
repair orders on guarantee	recall costs

non-receipt of goods

product or service quality

incorrect goods received

meeting statutory requirements

Most organizations monitor criteria of this nature but few publish the information. One rather useful study which attempted to relate this kind of criterion with training was that by Massey (1957). He described a programme of Post Office training and showed that the number of misdeliveries and errors (as well as absence without reporting and abuse of sick leave) decreased in the trained group when compared with an 'untrained' group.

The word 'constituents' can also be used to describe groups within the organization as these are, of course interdependent in some ways. Assessment of satisfaction will then mean asking the question, 'How do others value what we do?'. Ford Europe used this procedure in an organizational development programme. In 1981, faced with a major threat by Japanese manufacturers, Ford decided to improve the effectiveness of their European operation. The top 200 managers were brought together for a few days and were grouped by function—Production, Marketing, Personnel, etc. They were asked to comment on how the other functions helped or hindered their work. Thus the senior production managers worked in a room writing on flip-charts what it was that another function (e.g. Personnel) did that was helpful to them and what they did that hindered them. This was repeated for all the other functions. The other functions also wrote up their opinions. The second phase of the workshop was to reorganize the paper so that each function had a room which was papered with the views of others about them. For instance, the Personnel managers would go back to their room to find all the positive remarks from all the other functions on one of their walls, and all the negative ones on another wall (or two!). A good deal of the information generated had not been previously available and it was found to be useful. The managers started to think about ways in which the functions could make greater contributions to organizational effectiveness. The workshop then proceeded with some facilitation of intergroup processes and a greater commitment to other groups and the organization (rather than the parent function) was generated.

Internal processes

Using this approach, effective organizations are defined as those in which there is little internal strain, little intergroup conflict, where members feel integrated with the system and where information flows smoothly. Assessment of effectiveness may be against hard data like turnover of employees, absence, sick leave, etc.; often it is also against surveyed opinions of 'how we were' or 'how we would like to be'. The feeling of belonging and commitment often predisposes people to put in extra effort to achieve organizational goals. At the group level this used to be called morale. Although the word now sounds old-fashioned the concept is still important. It can sometimes be assessed by measuring such things as:

- Whether the staff believe that effort will be rewarded
- The motivating climate
- Job involvement

- Job satisfaction
- Group cohesiveness

Measures of these kinds of attitudes were the main interest of the organizational development movement which was so powerful in the USA during the 1970s, and many survey instruments have been developed by consultants and researchers. Useful sources of these inventories are the books by Henerson, Morris and Fitzgibbon (1978), Cook *et al.* (1981), and Seashore *et al.* (1982).

Poor morale may show in the statistics of:

transfer/turnover   disciplinary actions
absenteeism   grievances
medical visits   stoppages
accident rates   excessive work breakdown

If they are prevalent, such things can be expensive. Mirvis and Macy (1982) estimate the cost of one day's absence as US$80.06, that of turnover of an employee at US$160.65 and that of a grievance at US$54.52 (all at 1976 values).

Training can have a marked impact upon the patterns of work within parts of the organization, for instance, by increasing the quality of decision-making, of planning, or of supervision. Training can help to improve working within groups and between groups. It can also help people to cope with reduced staff levels and with managing time better. Many of these activities can affect the attitudes of managers and staff and these changes may affect the statistics associated with low morale.

The Prospect Foods Ltd group consists of nine catering, food and beverage companies operating in North Yorkshire. The problem was seen as being gaps in the staffs ability and willingness to take the intiative in spotting opportunities and solving problems. One day off the job training was organized and an important ingredient was the way participants from the various sites were mixed together with customers for group activities. The benefits have been a greater sense of involvement and a higher degree of confidence, resulting in many more members of staff being willing to take the initiative.

Source: National Training Awards 1988, The Training Agency

We hope that this rather detailed description and these examples have given you something of the flavour of the four categories of effectiveness. We suggest that you try to use the matrix in Figure 8.2 by mapping onto it the changes in effectiveness which you might expect from a particular programme. These can be at the level of the individual, the group or one of the higher levels (the higher the better). The changes might be expected in more than one category of effectiveness. We have found this exercise to be useful when discussing with line managers exactly what is supposed to change as a result of a training programme and how this change is to be measured. This, as you will remember, was thought likely to be one of the problems when trying to use the training model which is shown in Figure 1.3 (p 5).

It is interesting, as a theoretical exercise, to attempt some mapping of possible changes for courses which are already running. We suggest that you try for yourselves with a programme which is designed for individuals at a certain level in the organization—e.g. principles of management for junior managers, and then again with a programme which is 'tailor-made' for improving the effectiveness of a particular individual or group at work. What criteria can you measure? Which kind of programme do you find easier to evaluate?

Returning to the subject of the first part of this book, training as an effective process, we would argue that something like this matrix should be used to focus attention on results. Before the programme is designed, we should be planning where the changes in effectiveness are likely to occur and how we intend to measure them. Before an individual or group is accepted for training we should be planning what will change as a result of training.

9 Costing changes

This section on evaluating changes would not be complete without some mention of costing, cost-effectiveness and cost benefit analysis. Although few trainers carry out detailed costing activities, some flavour of what is involved in relating costs to results is useful when thinking through the logic of an evaluation. Some of the words which we have been using have rather different definitions when applied to costs and benefits and it is worth while stating these to set the scene:

- Improving efficiency means achieving the same results with lower costs
- Improving effectiveness means achieving better results with the same costs
- It is possible to get better results with lower costs and this is called improved productivity

Costing

Costing systems vary from one organization to another and liaison with the accounting department is usually necessary to make sure that the system adopted for training costs is compatible with other costing systems within the organization. A simple matrix for costing training events is shown in Figure 9.1.

	Personnel	Facilities	Equipment
Design	1(a)	1(b)	1(c)
Delivery	2(a)	2(b)	2(c)
Evaluation	3(a)	3(b)	3(c)

Figure 9.1 *Costing training events*

Design   The cost of design can be spread over the life of the programme (i.e. shared by the proposed number of programmes) as it will otherwise account for some 50 per cent of the overall costs. As a rough guideline, technical courses will need some five hours' preparation per hour of delivery. Programmed or packaged instruction will be much more expensive as up to 100 hours of design are needed for one hour of instruction. With computer-based learning the ratio can be as high as 400 : 1. The cost of designing the learning event will include things like:

1(a) Costs of preliminary analysis of training needs, development of objectives, course development, lesson planning, programming, audio-visual aids production, consultant advice, contractors.

1(b) Offices, telephones.

1(c) Production of workbooks, slides, tapes, tests, programmes, printing and reproduction.

Delivery   The cost of actually running the event will include:

2(a) Some proportion of annual salaries of trainers, lecturers, trainees, clerical/administration staff; costs of consultants and outside lecturers; travel costs.

2(b) Cost of conference centres or up-keep of classrooms, buildings, offices; accommodation and food; office supplies and expenses.

2(c) Equipment for delivering the training—slide projectors, videos, computers, simulators, workbooks, maintenance and repair of aids; expendable training materials or some proportion of cost relative to lifetime; handouts; hire of films, videos, etc.

Evaluation   The cost of evaluation is usually low compared to the other two elements. Probable costs include:

3(a) Cost of designing questionnaires, etc., follow-up interviews, travel, accommodation; analysis and summary of data collected; delivering the evaluation report.

3(b) Offices, telephones.

3(c) Tests, questionnaires, postage.

To give a complete picture it is also worth considering a general overhead for the expense of maintaining the training department. This may be allocated to individual training programmes on the basis of hours of participant learning, tutor involvement and level of administration required.

Salaries of trainees are often not allocated to training costs on the basis that a certain amount of 'slack' is necessary for effectiveness. For instance, when a foreman is taken off the factory floor a few hours a week to discuss supervisory methods, it makes very little difference to his 'output' as a foreman. In such a case it seems wrong to include the value of his salary for the hours spent as a cost to training. However, in the survey reported by Weinstein and Kasl (1982), the salary of trainees averaged about a third of all training costs. If this is the case for a programme which is being planned, then it seems worth while to account for it and use it as a criterion when deciding training priorities.

Cost-effectiveness comparisons

Cost-effectiveness analysis allows us to cost programmes and use this as a basis for comparing them. Usually an assumption is made that the level of effectiveness of the programmes will be similar and thus the cheaper, more efficient, form of delivery would be chosen. It is, of course, also possible to compare the effectiveness of the programmes and then offer a rationale for deciding whether the increased effectiveness of one programme justifies the extra cost. This comparison is more convincing when pilot versions of the two programmes can be run, so that actual, rather than estimated, levels of effectiveness can be used. An example might help your understanding of what is involved:

One of the High Street clearing banks was interested to compare the use of computer-based learning with delivering a traditional five-day off the job programme. The course was designed to teach some aspects of banking connected with lending money on mortgages. It was a knowledge-based programme and some of it was at the 'analytic' level, i.e. analysing a situation so that the correct procedure can be selected (see p 39). The CBL package was produced and, in piloting, it was found that the average trainee could complete it in three days. It was intended that the three days would be spent in the branch at which the trainee worked or one very close to it, and that the learning should be spaced at regular intervals during slack periods.

Costings were made for the development, delivery and evaluation of the CBL method. The delivery aspect was rather provisional as it was not known just how much co-ordination would be necessary for it to work well. (One of the problems with open-learning systems is to achieve the amount of structure which is necessary to allow the trainees to develop their learning in a systematic way. An hour or so here and there does not produce optimum learning.) The traditional five-day course had been running for some time and could be costed accurately. The development costs were spread over the numbers of people likely to be trained in three years. It was thus possible to make a comparison on the basis of estimated cost per student trained on each of the systems.

The systems could also be compared on an estimate of effectiveness:

• Shorter training time and less time away from work on the CBL system
• Less travel time and expense for the CBL users
• Less covering costs for trainees on the CBL package
• Better learning gain on the CBL package
• Some increment in computer literacy among staff using the CBL

A further basis for comparison of effectiveness would be the preference of the trainees for the methods being offered. Some would, no doubt, like to get away from the workplace for five days. Some would like to learn with others. There may also be some benefit in their discussing how work is organized differently in other branches.

Cost benefit analysis

In cost benefit analysis the intention is to discover whether the benefits from training are more valuable to the organization than the cost of the training. Whenever possible benefits are translated into monetary terms. Many products of training can be costed:

• Product benefits like increased volume or quality of product
• System benefits like increased productivity or efficiency, reduced job induction training time
• 'Hygiene' benefits like reduced turnover, absenteeism, strikes, etc.
• Reduction in accidents (perhaps costs which are inherent when not training)

A good example of a cost benefit study of a training activity is that by Woodward (1975), which we described earlier, using supervisors attending a NEBSS course. The average cost of the programme per supervisor was £887 and the average project benefit was calculated at

£2576, i.e. a benefit–cost ratio of 2.9 : 1. There are not many cost benefit studies of supervisory or management training in the literature; it is significant that we have to go back to 1975 for a good piece of work. This may be because the logic of the cost benefit approach is not very convincing when applied to the development of a manager.

> **Quality awareness programmes have become very popular and some of these lend themselves to cost benefit studies. For instance, Girobank decided to focus on improving quality in its Operations Directorate which undertakes most of the processing and data capture functions at the main operational site. A one-day quality awareness module was developed and delivered through 69 workshops. An internal publicity campaign maintained the impetus of the process. There has been a 22 per cent reduction in keying errors, a 28 per cent reduction in stationery re-order, and a reduction in the scrutiny of customer transaction documents. The estimated saving is about £1 million from an investment of £25,000 in training.**
>
> *Source:* National Training Awards for 1988, The Training Agency

Costing, cost benefit analysis and cost-effectiveness analysis are rather complex fields and we have no space here to do them justice. Interested readers are referred to Kearsley (1982) which is a useful introductory text and which includes a bibliography for further reading. If you really wish to carry out such an analysis, you might also look at the Cascio (1982) approach.

Value added employees

The logic underlying cost benefit analysis is not particularly appropriate to training and development activities because the benefits are rather diffuse and take some time to be realized. A more compelling logic is to be found in considering the process as one of adding value to employees. Before training, they are considered to need extra skills, knowledge, flexibility or whatever, in order to be able to work more effectively. After training they should be able to perform better and thus be of greater value to the organization. It should be possible to attribute some of this added value to the investment in training.

The value added approach has some assumptions underlying it which we will attempt to make explicit in our description. The first assumption is to take a rather simple definition of performance at work. There is an extensive literature on why some people perform well and others do not. The complexity of the literature is increased by the inclusion of the concept of motivation; there are many theories about what encourages or discourages good performance.

For the purpose of value added accounting we need a simple theory of performance. One way in which we can achieve this is to take a simple combination of the three major elements which appear again and again in theoretical approaches. These are:

1 There is a need for some ability or *skills* in areas which are relevant to the work

2 There must be some *motivation* to do the job (this may stem from the job context or the individual)
3 There must be the *opportunity* to use the skills and actually perform the job

As a simple equation this can be expressed as:

Performance = Some function of (Skills × Motivation × Opportunity)

The implication of the multiplication signs is that, if there is no skill, or motivation or opportunity, the performance will be zero.

This is a rather simple equation for a very complex concept. We have not attempted to state just what 'function' is involved, we have not said how we will decide which skills are relevant, nor have we attempted to operationalize 'motivation'. However, it is sometimes useful in social science to work with a 'primitive' concept which is inherently somewhat vague and imprecise, as this can make it possible to integrate seemingly disparate ideas. Certainly, with our present state of knowledge, it is not possible to produce a 'derived' concept which is precise, can be operationalized, and which integrates the widely differing theories of motivation and performance which are to be found in the literature.

Value added accounting begins with a pre-training analysis which esti-mates the position of the individual with respect to the average level of skill and of motivation of employees who are doing that kind of work. The scaling is done against a set of proportions:

• The middle 40 per cent are considered to be about average
• Those who are *noticeably* above average will represent about 25 per cent
• Those are *noticeably* below average will also comprise 25 per cent
• Those who are *outstandingly* good will be about 1 in 20, i.e. 5 per cent
• Those who are *outstandingly* bad will also comprise about 5 per cent

These proportions have been deliberately chosen because they force the distribution of skills or motivation into a 'normal' statistical distribution, with the mid-points of the bands close to whole standard deviations. This is shown diagrammatically in Figure 9.2.

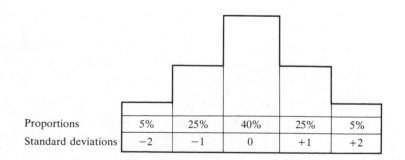

Proportions	5%	25%	40%	25%	5%
Standard deviations	−2	−1	0	+1	+2

Figure 9.2 *Normal distribution of ability*

One standard deviation (SD) above or below the mean will give a *noticeable* difference. Two SDs above or below the mean is the statistical criterion of an *outstanding* event—a significant difference.

It is possible, and for our purposes desirable, to transpose this scale of SDs into one which has 1 as its mean value. This will allow us to multiply average skills in the job by average motivation and, assuming that opportunity is available, to grade average performance as 1. Keeping the same relative value gives centre points of the intervals 0.33, 0.67, 1, 1.33, and 1.67, i.e.

Proportions	5%	25%	40%	25%	5%
Standard deviations	−2	−1	0	+1	+2
Transposed scale	0.33	0.67	1	1.33	1.67

The transposed values are plotted on the matrix shown in Figure 9.2 which shows the effect of multiplying estimated level of skills by esti-mated level of motivation to give an estimated level of performance.

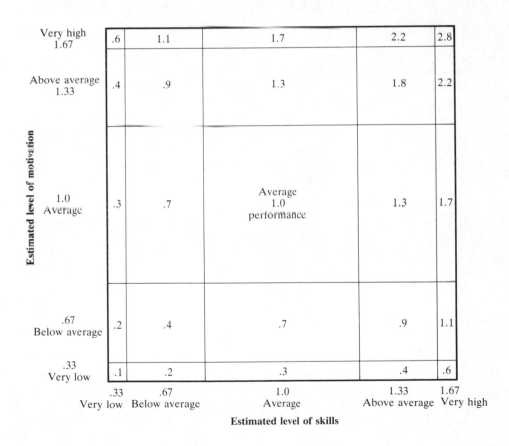

Figure 9.3 *Estimated levels of performance (assuming opportunity)*

Inspection of Figure 9.3 should clarify the logic of the value added approach. For instance, an employee who is considered to have average motivation (1.0) but whose skills are noticeably below average (0.67) is estimated to be performing at 0.7 of what is expected in the job. If training can bring such a person up to the average level of skills, the increment in performance is 0.3 and the value added to the employee by such training is, therefore, 0.3 of the salary for the job.

Employees who are noticeably below average on both skills and motivation are obviously being estimated as having a very low level of performance. It may be that training is not the answer for such people and that they may be better employed in some other kind of work. Employees who are noticeably above average or who are considered to be outstanding might also be considered for redeployment. It may well be that the company could benefit from giving them a more responsible job.

Training is often aimed at improving skills or motivation. The logic of the value added approach would suggest that if it is considered that employees have the skills but their motivation is low, then the training investment should be on supervisory and management training. If employees are thought to have the motivation but to lack some important skills, then the investment should be on employee skills training.

There are some important assumptions underlying all of this. Three of them need particular care:

1 Can managers allocate people to these proportions? Some managers believe that all their people are above average. Many have great difficulty with trying to measure people on a scale of motivation.
2 Is there the opportunity to use the skills and the encouragement to maintain motivation when new skills are being used? If the *opportunity* is not available, the whole logic collapses.
3 Are the skills which are required for successful job performance being identified accurately, and are they those which are being learned in training?

If these assumptions can be accepted, the approach can be used to estimate the return on training investment. The estimate can also be used for forward planning of training investment. Suppose that it is intended to offer training and group facilitation to introduce group and individual target setting which is related to the business plan. The intention would be to improve motivation and increase the opportunity to use the skills available. If this were to move most of the people who were previously considered average above the norm, either on skills or motivation, the benefit to the organization would be enormous.

Cost benefit accounting, which aims to summarize all of the outcomes in monetary terms, usually leaves out many of the things which are important because they cannot be converted into hard cash. Value added calculations have the advantage of usually being only a part of the evaluation. The evaluation report describes the outcomes in their own terms and a conclusion is then drawn that these do (or do not) imply a significant increase in skills and/or motivation. The section of the report which deals with costs can then include a value added calculation which indicates that there has been some return on the investment.

PART THREE

Strategies of evaluation

Introduction   In the previous two parts of this book we have discussed how to evaluate the process by which training is delivered and how to measure the changes which are expected to result from it. Now we turn to the more political aspects of evaluation: the various purposes which it can serve and the different approaches through which these purposes can be met. Before we become too deeply involved in this, it would be worth while for you to consider what your views are with respect to evaluation. What sort of process do you think that it should be? Figure P3.1 offers a set of seven point scales with anchors at each end. We suggest that you select a point on each scale line which represents your position with regard to the process of evaluation.

Evaluation of training should be:

Helping the management to inspect training	1	2	3	4	5	6	7	Helping the trainers to develop activities
An assessment process which leads to recommendations	1	2	3	4	5	6	7	Non-judgemental and therefore likely to pose questions
Statistical and scientific as its primary concern is with objective measurement	1	2	3	4	5	6	7	Anecdotal and descriptive as its primary concern is with subjective interpretation
A carefully planned process with a set agenda	1	2	3	4	5	6	7	Changing throughout as the focus changes during the process

Figure P3.1   *Views on the process of evaluation* (to be continued overleaf)

Estimating the worth of training activities to the organization	1	2	3	4	5	6	7	Providing feedback to the training department
Based on large samples and asking quite simple questions	1	2	3	4	5	6	7	Based on small samples and using in-depth questioning
Part of the process for all training activities	1	2	3	4	5	6	7	Carried out only when there is some doubt about a programme

Figure P3.1   (cont'd.)

The left-hand side of these scales represents a view that the main purpose of evaluation is to assess the worth of training to the organization and that this is best done by quantitative methods. The right-hand side is quite close to research on methods of learning where the quality of the experience, as reported by those involved, is the main focus. Many trainers can see the value of both these positions and hope that evaluation will satisfy both purposes. As we shall see, this is difficult to achieve. Particular forms of evaluation can be designed to meet particular purposes but it is necessary to be clear about what the purpose is before embarking on the process.

10 Purposes for evaluation

The most common view of evaluation is that it completes the cycle of training. Our view would be that it is integral to the cycle and has the key role of quality control of the cycle by providing feedback on:

- the effectiveness of the methods being used
- the achievement of the objectives set by both trainers and trainees
- whether the needs originally identified, both at organizational and individual level, have been met

It should be clear, from what we have already said about the training process and by inspection of the cycle in Figure 10.1, that the criteria against which to evaluate need to be established before the design of the learning situations.

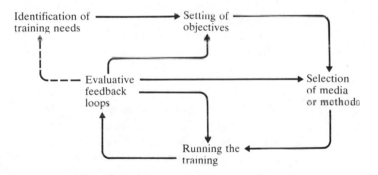

Figure 10.1   *The training cycle*

Goldstein (1986) defines evaluation as: 'The systematic collection of descriptive and judgemental information necessary to make effective decisions related to the selection, adoption, value and modification of various instructional activities.' We think this definition particularly valuable as it implies that evaluation is a set of information-gathering techniques. And further, that the selection of a particular strategy or technique, or of the particular aspect of the learning process which is examined, will vary with the purpose for which the evaluation is intended. Various purposes have been proposed by different authors.

Easterby-Smith (1986) offers three general purposes for evaluation: proving, improving and learning.

Proving aims 'to demonstrate conclusively that something has happened as a result of training or developmental activities'.

Improving implies 'an emphasis on trying to ensure that either the current or future programmes and activities become better than they are at present'.

Learning recognizes that 'evaluation cannot be divorced from the processes on which it concentrates . . . and is an integral part of the learning and development process itself'.

We have chosen a rather more complex grouping of five main categories:

Feedback

Feedback evaluation provides quality control over the design and delivery of training activities. Feedback to the participants during training will be an essential part of the learning process. Timely feedback to the trainers about the effectiveness of particular methods and about the achievement of the objectives set for the programme will help in the development of the programme currently being run and those planned for future occasions. The information which needs to be collected for feedback evaluation is:

- the extent to which the objectives are being or have been met
- before and after measures of levels of knowledge, concepts used, skills, attitudes and behaviour
- sufficient detail about content to be able to estimate the effectiveness of each topic covered during the learning event and each learning situation
- evidence of transfer of learning back to the workplace
- some identification of those for whom the programme was of most and of least benefit so that the target population can be more closely defined

The main purpose of what we are calling feedback evaluation is the development of learning situations and training programmes to improve what is being offered. There is a secondary aspect, for identifying what is good and what is not so good improves the professional ability of members of the training department. Reports based on feedback evaluation tend to have conclusions in them which the training department can consider and act on (or not act on) as appropriate.

Control

Control evaluation relates training policy and practice to organizational goals. There could also be a concern for the value to the organization of the contribution and costs of the training function. Careful control evaluation might also answer questions like, 'Will a main focus on training give a better solution to the problem than re-structuring the department or re-designing some of the jobs?' The information required for control evaluation is therefore:

- that which is required for feedback (as listed above)
- some measures of the worth of the output of the training to the organization
- some measures of cost

- some attempt at a comparative study of different combinations of methods for tackling the problem

Control evaluation is quite close to the left-hand side of the scales in Figure P3.1. It is something that an organization might require of a training manager or might impose through the creation of a group which is responsible for evaluating but is not part of the training func- tion—an evaluation cell. There is a strong tendency for this kind of evalu- ation to result in a report which is full of recommendations, some of which will require changes to be made.

Research

Research evaluation seeks to add to knowledge of training principles and practice in a way which will have more general application than feedback evaluation. Studies of ways in which people learn or studies of factors which facilitate transfer would be examples. Research evaluation can also serve to improve the techniques available for other purposes like feedback, control and intervention.

Research evaluation is particularly concerned with issues of validity of which there are two types. Internal validity may be defined as the extent to which particular conclusions may justly be drawn from the data. The data should be derived from a carefully controlled situation with good experimental design so that alternative explanations can be ruled out. External validity is defined as the extent to which conclusions drawn from the experimental situation may be applicable generally to other situations.

Research evaluation into training within organizations is particularly diffi- cult as there is seldom the opportunity to set up a well-designed project with true control groups and time series of observations. Consequently there are not many examples in the literature.

Intervention

It is an illusion to believe that the process of evaluation is able to apply some objective measuring instrument external to and independent of the programme being evaluated. The evaluation will almost inevitably affect the way in which the programme is viewed and can be used to redefine the sharing of responsibility for the learning between the trainers, trainees and employing managers. Planned intervention through evaluation can:

- involve the line manager in the pre- and post-measurement
- involve the line manager in the extension of training after the event by debriefing and helping with the implementation of the action plan
- change the way in which the employing managers select and brief people before the learning event
- cause the training department to rethink the deployment of trainers to functions within the organization and strengthen the liaison role

It can thus be a powerful method of intervening into the human resource procedures within an organization.

The organizational change literature includes many interesting descriptions of the ways in which consultants have changed the ways in which things are done in organizations merely by being present. Perhaps the best known of these is the so-called Hawthorne studies where the presence of researchers, who were interested in the workforce and what they were doing, had the effect of increasing the volume of work. We recently had a similar experience in a large UK industrial organization. We were brought in as consultants to the central personnel services who were trying to persuade the various regional training groups to evaluate their training. Our contract implied that we were to advise on methods by which the organization could evaluate various types of training. It rapidly emerged that we were making an important contribution by simply going into the various regions around the country and talking about evaluation and its relationship to organizational effectiveness. The informal communications network of regional training managers began to buzz with questions about evaluation and individual managers began to ask themselves questions which they had not asked before. They also became convinced that head office considered the issue to be important (otherwise why would they hire an external consultant?). A number of evaluative studies were started with no more input from us than a request for a date to talk to the regional training manager!

Power games

Perhaps all information is potentially powerful but certainly evaluative information about training events can be used within the organization in a political way. As it is probably not possible to avoid these power games, perhaps it is not desirable to aim to do so. It does, however, place a responsibility on the evaluator to make sure that the evidence which is being used is based upon a sound study. People who would be described as 'negativists' by Randall (1960) make up their minds on anecdotal evidence and are by no means rare. For instance, much of the bad press which sensitivity training received was at the level of 'Did you hear about what happened on the . . . programme last week?'

11 Approaches to evaluation

Goal-based evaluation

Evaluation in its modern form has developed from attempts to improve the educational process, particularly that in the United States. Measurement and assessment of people became popular at about the same time as scientific management and school officials began to see the possibility of applying these concepts to school improvement.

The most influential early work was that of Tyler who was appointed in 1932 to be the research director to the eight-year study which was intended to compare the value of progressive high school curricula with more conventional ones. Tyler's main contribution was to insist that the curricula needed to be organized by the use of objectives. Objectives were seen as being critical because they were the basis for planning, for guiding the instruction, and for the preparation of test and assessment procedures. They were also the basis on which a systematic evaluation of a programme could be designed. As he put it (1950):

'The process of evaluation is essentially the process of determining to what extent the educational objectives are actually being realized . . . however, since educational objectives are essentially changes in human beings, that is, the objectives aimed at are to produce certain desirable changes in the behaviour patterns of the students, then evaluation is the process for determining the degree to which these changes in behaviour are actually taking place.'

The process of evaluation proposed by Tyler had a number of phases as follows:

1 Collect, from as wide a consultation as possible, a pool of objectives which might be related to the curriculum.
2 Screen the objectives carefully to select a subset which covers the desirable changes.
3 Express these objectives in terms of the student behaviours which are expected.
4 Develop instruments for testing each objective. These must meet acceptable standards of objectivity, reliability and validity.
5 Apply the instruments before and after learning experiences.
6 Examine the results to discover strengths and weaknesses in the curriculum.
7 Develop hypotheses about reasons for weaknesses and attempt to rectify these.
8 Modify the curriculum and recycle the process.

Tyler's approach was a distinct advance over existing assessment systems which were based upon judgements about the progress of individual students. These judgements were usually based upon examination results and teachers' impressions of classroom work, but there was little attempt to standardize these in such a way that sound comparisons between programmes could be drawn. Educational staff understood the rationale of Tyler's process and valued the way in which it made explicit what it was that they were trying to do.

Training in organizations took some time to catch up with educational practice. It was not until the late 1960s and early 1970s that organizations started to control the quality of training by setting training objectives. Two distinct strands can be identified:

1 the behavioural objectives approach which developed from programmed instruction, and
2 variations on the theme of setting goals to be achieved within the training, after the training activity and longer-term.

The *behavioural objectives* approach is associated with the work of Mager (1962) but the principles are based upon the work of Skinner (1954).

A goal-based strategy for controlling and evaluating training was adopted by the British Army in 1968. The skills required for successful performance of each of the Army employments were analysed and recorded as behavioural objectives. Training for each 'employment' (the word essentially means 'technical trade') was then designed to meet these objectives. The job analyses showed that some objectives were only necessary for more experienced tradesmen and thus it was possible to structure the training courses at a number of levels (usually three). The process of defining the trade levels in terms of behavioural objectives required a great deal of effort, but it proved to be very successful in improving the effectiveness and efficiency of the training. The main reasons for this success were:

- The objectives were based upon performance derived from the initial analysis of the job and there was no problem in transferring the training.
- Making explicit what the training objectives were removed a good deal of training which had previously been given on the basis of the trainers' ideas of what might be useful.
- The use of the objectives directed the attention of the trainees to what was considered important and allowed them to set learning goals for themselves. Research on adult motivation suggests this is a sound procedure (see, for instance, Locke *et al.* (1981)) which is likely to improve performance.

Courses where technicians were improving their qualifications and thus their earning power, and where they were given a set of behavioural objectives which specified what was required of them, were quite different in nature from the previous, instructor-led, programmes. The role of the trainers became one of providing a resource to supply help when asked. The trainees took on much of the responsibility and actually trained themselves.

There were some problems with this for trainers who were technical experts. Many of them had enjoyed demonstrating their skills and felt that their talents were not being used properly in the newer, more learner-centred form of training.

This approach advocates the control of training by the setting of objectives which specify performances which can be demonstrated, conditions under which these performances will be tested, and the standards which will be acceptable. The trainees are offered these detailed objectives as goals and evaluation is a matter of adding up the numbers attained by individuals and groups.

An example of behavioural training objective is given in Figure 11.1. Some feel that such objectives are trivial and cannot capture the richness of the job context. This may be true but, as can be seen by the example, they offer a comprehensive method for describing a procedure, when a procedure is appropriate, and when it is inappropriate.

Training Objective No. ....

1 Performance:
   Overtake a moving vehicle
2 Test conditions:
   (a) In any vehicle less than 3 tons unladen weight
   (b) On a public road
   (c) In daylight
   (d) Accompanied by the examiner
3 Test standards:
   (a) Safely, without danger or inconvenience to other road users
   (b) Smoothly
   (c) In the appropriate gear for the conditions and speeds
   (d) Judge distances, gaps and relative speeds adequately
   (e) Carry out correct sequences as in para 4(a) below
4 Learning points:
   (a) Sequence of action by driver
       (i)   Check mirrors
       (ii)   Signal
       (iii) Select correct gear
       (iv)   Check mirrors
       (v)   Pull out if clear ahead
       (vi)   Cancel signal
       (vii) Overtake
       (viii) Signal intention of coming in
       (ix)   Resume correct road position when safe to do so
       (x)   Cancel signal
       (xi)   Change into top gear (if nec)
   (b) Restrictions on overtaking
       (i)   Narrow road, bends
       (ii)   Power/size of own vehicle
       (iii) Double white lines
       (iv)   Brows of hills

Figure 11.1   *A behavioural training objective* (to be continued overleaf)

(v)   Urban areas—pedestrian crossings, junc-
        tions, parked vehicles, etc. (see Highway
        Code)
(vi)   Speed limits not to be exceeded
(c) Overtaking on the left
(i)   When turning left, vehicle in front turning
        right, one-way streets
(ii)   Explain 'filtering'

Figure 11.1   (cont'd.)

A large portion of many jobs can be described at this procedural level
as we discovered when considering how to measure changes in knowledge (p 39) and changes in levels of skills (p 46). The objective also
contains a clear statement of how achievement will be measured and
this greatly simplifies the evaluation. Evaluation becomes an integral
part of the training process as trainees are continually involved in a
cycle—testing achievement, target-setting, learning and re-testing.

A later development in the use of objectives to control training has been
to specify the expected outcomes as objectives at a number of levels. The
first important contribution to this approach was that of Kirkpatrick (1959),
who argued that objectives should be set for the *reactions* of the trainees
to the programme, for *learning* at the end of the programme, for
changed *behaviour* in the job, and for *ultimate* changes in organizational
effectiveness. Others followed this general framework but offered rather
different categories. Figure 11.2 is an attempt to cross classify the better
known approaches. The framework in the columns on the left is a
commonsense chronological one based upon the cycle of learning during
training, which then applies this in the workplace.

The most comprehensive of these frameworks is that offered by
Hamblin (1974). He argues that learning should, as far as possible, be
evaluated in terms of pre-defined objectives. He differs from the
behavioural objectives school in acknowledging that there may be situations when it is neither desirable nor possible to define the objectives
in detail. The five levels of evaluation are linked by a cause and effect
chain:

	Training
leads to	*Reactions*
which lead to	*Learning*
which lead to	*Changes in behaviour*
which lead to	*Changes in the organization*
which lead to	*Change in the achievement of ultimate goals*

My experience as an evaluator indicates that many courses are monitored only at the reactions level and that the main objective is that the
trainees should enjoy themselves. Hamblin argues that the reactions
measured during and at the end of the programme should meet pre-
specified objectives which indicate attitude change rather than just
enjoyment. Trainers should be specifying in what ways they are hoping
that the trainees will react.

Areas	Components	Kirkpatrick (1959)	Warr, Bird Rackham (1970)	Glossary (1971)	Hamblin (1974)
Within the training	• Judgements of the quality of trainees experiences • Feedback to trainees about learning	Reactions	Reactions		Reactions
	• Measures of gain or change • Feedback to trainers about methods	Learning	Immediate	Internal validation	Learning
At the job after training	• Relevance of the learning goals			External validation	
	• Measures of use of learning or change of behaviour • Retrospective back to trainers	Behaviour	Inter-mediate		Job behaviour
Organizational effectiveness	• Measures of change in organizational performance • Implementation of individual/action plans or projects	Results	Ultimate	Evaluation	Organization
Social or cultural values	• Measures of social cost and benefits • Human resources accounting			Evaluation	Ultimate Ultimate

Figure 11.2 *Levels at which objectives can be set*

Learning—defined as: 'acquiring the ability to behave in new kinds of ways'—should be evaluated against job behaviours of the trainees, and job behaviour objectives should be descriptive of what successful trainees are expected to do when back in post. The expected changes in job behaviour should be linked with changes in effectiveness of the organization, but Hamblin accepts that this is often an assumption. We have considered this problem above and argued that it can often be solved by setting objectives for changes lower down, in *parts* of the organization.

Ultimate goals are likely to be commercial in the private sector organizations, but in organizations like hospitals or schools, the quality of the service itself may form the ultimate goal. Objectives may consequently be product-orientated in the former and process-orientated in the latter.

The strategy which Hamblin is recommending is to select the level at which evaluation is required and then write down the objectives to be achieved at that level. The effects of training can then be evaluated up to that level. The chain can break down between any two levels, for instance, 'changes in the organization' which are attributable to the training programme will not occur if there are no 'changes in behaviour'.

The logic of this approach is compelling. Deciding what training is intended to achieve, pre-setting objectives to specify what effects should be seen, and then evaluating whether they have been achieved, is a sound way to ensure effective training. In practice it is often difficult to produce clear linkages between training content and job tasks, especially in management training. Although it is also difficult to link training objectives to organizational goals, we would support Hamblin in the view that it is worth trying.

We have spent some time discussing the history of goal-based evaluation and some of its limitations when applied to training and development activities occurring within organizations. The approach has great strengths and it is almost universally recommended by trainers and managers in organizations when they sponsor evaluations.

Goal-free evaluation

In 1957 the Russians launched their first Sputnik and this had a profound effect in America where the educational system was widely blamed for not producing equally imaginative citizens. In the search for new curricula the Americans found that the system of evaluation developed from Tyler's work did not help them. The most articulate criticism came from Cronbach (1963) who made three major points:

1 If evaluation was to be of use to course developers, it needed to focus attention on how decisions were made during the development of the programmes. The crucial questions are:
   (a) Who are the decision-makers?
   (b) What kinds of decisions do they make?
   (c) What criteria are they using?
2 Evaluation should focus on improving the course while it is still under development rather than appraising one already in use.
3 Evaluation used for developing a particular programme would be most useful if it focused on performance characteristics of that programme rather than on comparison with others.

Others soon followed Cronbach's lead, the most influential of them being Scriven (1967). Scriven identified two different types of evaluation: *formative* evaluation concerned with improving the programme, and *summative* evaluation concerned with judging its worth. He also argued that evaluation should not only be concerned with whether goals were achieved, but also whether the goals were *worth* achieving.

The most radical step came later when Scriven (1973) proposed that the evaluator should not set out to discover what the designers' objectives were. Objectives or goal-based evaluation will yield a measure of intent and that may not be all that that has been achieved. The evaluator measures what he or she expects to find and tends not to recognize, or value, unanticipated changes. The proposed, goal-free method would overcome this problem as the evaluator, deliberately unaware of the objectives for the programme, would set out to talk to participants about whether the programme had been of any benefit to them. It would thus be possible to pick up unintended effects as well as those expected by the programme organizers. The evaluator would thus produce two types of information: an assessment of the actual effects and a set of needs against which the importance of the effects could be evaluated.

In the main this model has remained at a conceptual level as its main advocate has not been very helpful in describing how goal-free evaluation should be translated into practice. For instance, how does one decide which effects to examine? How does one judge which opinions are valuable?

Thirty people are interviewed six months after a programme:

- **fifteen say that they enjoyed the programme**
- **two cannot remember anything about it**
- **one did not enjoy it because not enough cold drinks were available**
- **ten said that they thought that the programme had been useful to them**
- **two said that they now did things differently**

Was the programme a success? What criteria are you using? Do you think that someone else (not the cold drinks vendor) would use the same criteria?

Goal-free methods were rather overstated as a reaction to the ubiquity of goal-based evaluation. In fact, their value may well be in the ways in which they can complement rather than challenge that approach. Scriven has been able to convince evaluators that it is necessary to consider a wide range of effects rather than just those intended. Many evaluators now consider collecting qualitative data about what affects the participants' value as well as the quantitative information about numbers of objectives achieved.

Responsive evaluation

Part of the legacy of this discussion about goal-free evaluation versus that based upon pre-specified objectives was the growing conviction that evaluation was actually a political process, and that the various values held in society were not represented by an evaluative process which implied that consensus was possible.

The term 'responsive evaluation' was first used by Stake (1975) to describe a strategy in which the evaluator is less concerned with the objectives of the programme than with its effects in relation to the concerns of interested parties—the 'stakeholders'.

In conducting a responsive evaluation the evaluator first tries to identify the main clients. For a training programme these are likely to be the staff organizing the programme and a sample of those who will be affected by the programme (both trainees and line managers). The aim is to gain a sense of their different postures with regard to the programme and the purposes which each group has for the evaluation. The evaluator then makes personal observations of the programme to get a direct sense of what it is about. He or she has begun to discover the purpose of the programme, both stated and real, and also the concerns that various stakeholders may have. Now the evaluator is in a position to conceptualize the issues and problems which the evaluation should address.

The design of the evaluation takes place next. It should be noted that this is well into the process of evaluation. It cannot be designed before the evaluator can specify the kinds of data and information which will be needed to satisfy the various issues and concerns. The evaluator selects whichever methods and instruments are most appropriate and collects the data. The information collected is organized into themes and the evaluator matches issues and concerns to audiences in deciding what form the report will take (as there may be different reports for different audiences). It is worth noting the interactions implicit in this process; at any stage the evaluator may reformulate what is being done and there is no certain way of predicting the outcome of the evaluation.

There is no natural end point but simply a place convenient for reporting. Given sufficient time and budget the evaluator could recycle the entire evaluation process as a result of changes in the concerns of the stakeholders contingent on their receiving their reports.

Parlett and Hamilton (1977) describe a form of evaluation which has some similarities to responsive evaluation and recommend it for educational research. The primary concern of 'illuminative evaluation' is with description and interpretation rather than with measurement and prediction. The suggested method by which to achieve this is 'progressive focusing', which means the systematic reduction of the breadth of the enquiry to give more concentrated attention to the emerging issues. A key value which is apparent in the work of Parlett and Hamilton is that they reject the classical evaluator's stance of seeking an objective truth that is equally relevant to all of the parties in favour of acknowledging the diversity of questions posed by different interest groups.

Legge (1984) also arrives at a position which is quite close to that of responsive evaluation from a quite different route. She discusses the research on evaluation of planned organizational change and criticizes it on two main grounds. The first of these is that evaluation research which is rigorous enough to be acceptable to an academic is almost always too trivial to be useful to decision-makers as the designs are so restrictive that most of the factors which are of interest are controlled out. The second is that most of the research is so badly designed that it is unacceptable to an academic because threats to internal validity have not been controlled and there is little confidence in the conclusions drawn. Legge suggests that rather than attempting evaluation as rigorously controlled research, a 'contingent approach' be adopted. This essentially consists of asking the major stakeholders four major questions:

1 Do you want the proposed change programme to be evaluated?
2 What functions do you wish the evaluation to serve?
3 Which approach (of a number of possible alternatives) best matches the functional requirements of the evaluation exercise?
4 To what extent are constraints on the planning and implementation of

the change programme, which will be necessary because of this approach to evaluation, acceptable?

Responsive evaluation is gaining ground as the most favoured method for evaluating educational and social programmes in the USA. It has obvious strengths as a procedure for evaluating training and development activities within organizations because it attempts to take into account the interests of various groups rather than just the sponsors of the programme. It also has a rationale for collecting information—the needs of the various stakeholders.

Systems evaluation

Systems evaluation actually offers much less than meets the eye. The title suggests the analysis of the whole system and the relationships between subsystems. The purpose of such an analysis would be to improve the interfaces between the subsystems in such a way as to increase the effectiveness of the system. That is what 'systems approaches' set out to do. The most comprehensive description of the strategy of systems evaluation is to be found in the book by Rossi, Freeman and Wright (1979). What one discovers by reading this is that the questions which this strategy sets out to answer are:

- Is the programme reaching the target population?
- Is it effective?
- How much does it cost?
- Is it cost-effective?

These are questions posed by policy makers who are interested in 'the facts' and not in opinions; the problems with this approach are implicit in the collection of this kind of 'hard' data. The first question will be answered by defining the size of the target population and working out the proportion who have attended, i e 'reaching' is being defined in terms of attendance rather than useful learning. One might argue that to define 'reaching' in this way makes it a trivial criterion. 'Effectiveness' is difficult to measure in terms which satisfy those who want simple statistics. Such people are usually willing to accept statements of how many of the programme's objectives have been achieved. The programme's objectives are, of course, understood to be those of the sponsors of the programme. As we have seen above, they may not be representative of the objectives of other stakeholders.

Professional review

Most courses leading to professional recognition are approved by a committee which reviews evidence of what the course will contain and whether it reaches the desired standard. For instance, not all Bachelor degree courses in psychology offered in universities and polytechnics are recognized by the British Psychological Society. Recognition is given to those courses which cover the 'right ground' where this is defined by breadth of coverage and the amount of time devoted to subjects like experimental design and practical laboratory work. Graduates from recognized courses may join the BPS but others must first obtain other qualifications. This is what we are calling the professional review strategy.

This sort of approach can also be used within an organization to consider the relevance of a syllabus to organizational requirements and the breadth and quality of the programme. An informal variation of this is quite common; the training manager offers a particular programme and puts it into the brochure because he or she has carried out a 'professional review' of it.

It is our view that a more formal approach would be better. As a minimum:

• the review procedures need to be agreed by interested parties
• some consensus must be reached on the criteria for judgement
• the reviewing body needs to include some diversity of interests

This might well be an economic way of evaluating a training programme but there are likely to be some political problems. For one thing trainers, like most professional people, do not like to have others investigating the way in which they work.

Quasi-legal approach

Quasi-legal evaluation operates like a court of inquiry. Witnesses are called to testify and submit evidence. Great care is taken to hear a wide range of evidence (opinions, values and beliefs) from the organizers of the programme and the 'users' as well as the accountants. Such an approach has been used to evaluate social programmes but not, to our knowledge, for formally evaluating training or development activities sponsored by organizations. It might be suitable for such a purpose provided a sufficiently impartial 'judge' could be found and provided some agreement could be reached about who comprised the key witnesses.

Pre-programme evaluation

It is not uncommon in training to evaluate, in a rather informal way, a number of possible methods of structuring an activity before it is implemented. Given some information about the prospective target population, the objectives for the programme and the type of learning required, some decision criteria can be established for selecting a training design and the media to support it. Education technology books (e.g. Davies, 1971) and algorithms like CRAMP (Pearn, 1981) offer a variety of rationales for this selection.

Pre-programme evaluation goes a little further than this and asks whether the procedures being considered are likely to bring about the desired changes. Warr, Bird and Rackham (1970) call this 'input evaluation' and suggest that the following questions should be posed:

• What are the relevant merits of different training techniques?
• Is it feasible to run the training within the organization or will the services of some external agency be needed?
• Does the age or background of the trainees suggest any particular training method?
• How much time is likely to be available for training?
• What were the results last time a similar programme was run?

The organizational change literature on 'institutionalization' and 'routinization' of changes also provides some criteria which are necessary to carry out a pre-programme evaluation. For instance, Goodman and Dean (1982) focus on the factors which affect the persistence of a new policy or procedure which has been introduced as an intended change. They argue that institutionalization is a continuum which starts with knowledge of the change at one end and then goes through 'performance' and 'preference' to reach 'incorporation into norms and values' at the other. In order to assess where individuals and groups fall on this continuum it is necessary to examine five processes:

1 *Socialization*—the extent to which information is transmitted to organizational members about the required behaviours, etc.
2 *Commitment*—whether people are accepting the change by personal choice or because of external constraints.
3 *Reward allocation*—the extent to which rewards are related to desired behaviours.
4 *Diffusion*—the extent to which the new form is spreading to other parts of the organization.
5 *Sensing and calibration*—the extent to which feedback information, which can be used to take corrective action, is available.

The culture of the organization interacts with these five processes and it is against this that we might be able to predict whether or not the change is likely to be accepted into organizational procedures and thus survive in the longer term. If, for each of the five processes above, we ask perhaps a representative steering committee to estimate 'The extent to which it is likely that. . .', this should give an evaluation of the likely success of the programme before it is implemented. It should also alert the designers to some of the key issues which need to be addressed if good transfer is to be achieved.

The perceptive reader will feel a sense of *déjà vu* here as we have now come full circle. At the beginning of the book (see Figure 1.2 on page 4) we argued that these sorts of variables should be considered if the purpose of the training is to change the way in which things are done.

Objectivity of evaluation

Within all these methods it is possible to use different levels of analysis—individual, work groups, departments, inter-departments or overall organization. Usually it is necessary to attempt some synthesis of these levels when producing a balanced report. It should be obvious from this and from a consideration of the various strategies available that the evaluation will never produce the truth. The objectives approach will lead to the collection of relatively 'hard' data which can be reliably measured, but the evaluators will hold values which determine which objectives will be investigated and what evidence will be acceptable. Systems evaluation will also produce 'hard' data, but it has similar problems to the goal-based approach. The other approaches are more subjective in their methods of collecting data but attempt to get a wider 'truth'.

The objectivity within an evaluation comes from a conviction that if someone else had carried out the study he or she would have come to similar conclusions. As Professor Alec Rodger (the founder of the Occupational Psychology Department at Birkbeck College, University of London) used to say: 'A study should be technically sound, administratively convenient and politically defensible.' The evaluation will rarely be objective in the scientific sense of a passive observation of events. This is only possible when unobtrusive measures are being used (such as statistics on absence, or levels of production, or sales volume per number of visits). An evaluation will usually become part of the training process as the presence of the evaluator in a part of the organization will, to some extent, change the perceptions of a proportion of the people about some of the changes and objectives of the training activity.

Presenting an evaluation report

The final stage of most evaluations will be the presentation of the report. The extent to which this will be accepted and acted upon will depend to a large extent on what took place at the beginning of the study. It is crucial to identify the major stakeholders and to try to discover what agendas they have. Many of those who have a long-term interest in the programme will have strong views on the desired outcomes of the study. It is essential to keep such people informed during the evaluation and to involve them in key decisions if they are to 'own' and therefore act on the results. This is not to imply that the evaluator must produce the findings which the stakeholders are expecting; rather that their views must be incorporated and they must be kept informed. It is, of course, also essential to establish that the people receiving the report have the power to implement the changes being suggested.

One way of overcoming some of the problems in presenting the report is to discover what kind of report the major stakeholders expect. At the beginning of this part of the book, we asked you to decide what it was that you meant by evaluation. Making a decision on each of the scales in Figure P3.1, makes explicit what kind of process evaluation is thought to be. We suggest that, before embarking on an evaluation, you ask the major stakeholders to fill in a set of attitude scales like those in Figure P3.1. You will then know what kind of data they think that you ought to collect and something about how they expect you to present it. That should at least alert you to some of the problems if their views are very different from your own. In most cases we think that it will greatly assist in putting the case and helping them to make changes.

The nature of the report will, of course, reflect the purpose for which it is written, but generally it will contain most of the following sections:

1 A *summary* which is intended for those who will not have time to read the full report. Care should be taken to ensure that this is a balanced extract, as many people will not read (or remember) the supporting arguments in the main body of the report.
2 A statement of the *purpose* of the evaluation and how it was designed to meet that purpose.
3 A description of the *methods* used for data collection and a summary of the findings.

4 A summary of *costs*.

5 The *results* expressed in terms of increased individual and organizational benefits.

6 *Conclusions* drawn from the previous sections. These may sometimes be recommendations if the purpose of the evaluation requires these.

The way in which the findings are communicated during the study will depend upon organizational style. Some organizations prefer written memoranda, but in many the important decisions are actually made in face to face discussions. The presentation of the report itself is not the time to 'defend'. If there is some bad news, this should be brought to the attention of those concerned before the presentation.

An evaluation report will usually be a part of a change process and it is helpful to consider the method of change which is to be used. The literature on planned organizational change can help here, as a number of models for this process have been described.

One possible method is the *research, development and dissemination* model (Havelock, 1969). In this the research leads to a report which contains conclusions for further development. This report is widely circulated and the information so disseminated is acted on by the target audience. This model assumes that the recipients of the report are essentially passive consumers, that they are rational, and that they will see the importance of the changes and be willing to make them.

A second possibility is the *social interaction model* (Havelock, 1969). This is more sensitive to the relationships and processes which are involved in the dissemination phase. The users are seen as holding a variety of positions and as being likely to adopt attitudes and behaviour which vary with their reference group. This model implies that it is necessary to make face to face contacts with the different audiences and that the process is nearer one of negotiation than one of simple dissemination of information.

A third plausible method is the *planned change model* (Sashkin, Morris and Horst, 1973). Here data collection and research are shared between the change agent and the client. Information is considered useful only if it leads to action. The assumption is that change occurs through a continuous process of data generation, planning and implementation. The changes which are introduced need to be supported and 'routinized' if they are to be fully utilized.

The process and the purpose of the evaluation will vary in different organizations. What we are suggesting is that you should think about the process.

• Are you intending to produce conclusions or achieve change?

• What sort of target audience have you? Are they relatively passive and likely to accept the changes? Do the changes need to be negotiated?

• When do you withdraw from the scene? Should you continue to be involved as a change agent would be until the changes have become part of the routine?

Whatever method is adopted, a successful presentation of a report should result in action planning by the recipients. An effective report must contain information which the recipients will find meaningful as they are unlikely to introduce changes if they cannot understand the data or do not find it relevant to their problems. The information should also have some impact so that it can energize some change and be a stimulus for further action or investigation. It is worth emphasizing again that the report should be presented to those who have the ability to make necessary changes.

The problems of presenting evaluative reports has been rather neglected in the literature, but interesting discussions may be found in Patton (1978) and Easterby-Smith (1986). It is an area which the practitioner should not neglect.

12 Do you really want to evaluate your training?

Evaluation, if it is to become an integral part of the training and development activities as we have suggested, requires the expenditure of energy and time. Is it likely to be worth while? Perhaps a little quiz might help you to make the decision. Here are ten points for you to consider:

Q1 How are the trainees selected for the programme which you are thinking of?

   a We do not know
   b They, or their supervisors, feel that the programme would be good for them
   c The training will be of direct benefit in improving their ability to do a particular job (or part of it)

Q2 How are the trainees briefed before the programme?

   a They receive instructions sent out to them before they attend the course
   b We talk to them about their objectives at the beginning of the programme
   c They discuss with their line manager and a trainer exactly what learning will be available on the programme and how it is to be applied in the job

Q3 Most of our programmes are aimed at:

   a A group of people (like all junior managers doing a set topic like 'Principles of Management')
   b Individuals to increase personal knowledge and skills or change attitudes
   c Improving organizational results and effectiveness

Q4 Pre-programme evaluation or cost benefit comparisons of various methods of achieving changes are:

   a Virtually never done
   b Occasionally done for particularly important programmes
   c Frequently done, almost as a matter of course

Q5 How do your trainers get feedback on their performance?

   a They feel good when they have performed well
   b There are happiness sheets and discussions at the end of the course

    c They actually see that people are using in their jobs what they learned on the course

Q6   When a trainee returns to the workplace his or her supervisor:

    a Welcomes him or her back and gives extra work to make up for the time away

    b Asks if he or she had a good time and whether the course was well run

    c Requires a debrief on what has been learned and becomes actively involved in making opportunities to use the learning

Q7   Results of training programmes are communicated:

    a Only if requested

    b To the head of Personnel and sometimes to heads of other departments

    c On a routine basis to selected audiences

Q8   Training expenditure has to be justified by:

    a The training department

    b Heads of the various other departments

    c Line managers

Q9   Line management involvement in the delivery of training is:

    a Nil

    b A few heads of department introducing courses and a few specialists having some input

    c Common, more than half of the programmes having some input from line managers

Q10   At present the training department's impact on organizational effectiveness:

    a Cannot be assessed

    b Could be assessed but at great cost

    c Is estimated on a regular basis

Scoring: 1 for A, 2 for B, and 3 for C.

It is rather simplistic, but it could be argued that a score of below 20 indicates a training function which is divorced from organizational realities. Such a function could be at risk as it will be seen primarily as a cost to the organization. When money is tight, the organization can, and will, cut the budget for a training department which demonstrates its value by contributing 'n' person/days training per year. The organization cannot so easily cut a function which is manifestly contributing to organizational well-being and to increased effectiveness.

The costs of evaluation can be heavy and, if this is to be justified as an investment, some selection of programmes is indicated. Some training events are essentially social (for example, the one-day get-together where people from different functions meet and hear a series of briefings on the work of other parts of the organization). Evaluation of such events would hardly be worth the cost involved.

The importance of the programme is a further criterion for consideration. Usually evaluation of one-off programmes would not be considered worth while. However, if the programme is intended to help with the solution of some important problem then evaluation is indicated. Similarly, if the consequences of not ensuring that the training has been effective (for instance, with safety training) are important, then evaluation should be considered.

Evaluation *should* be required of *any* organizational activity which represents a significant investment of funds. Traditionally this has not been required of the training department, but it is becoming increasingly common for senior managers to discuss the need for training and development to contribute to business performance.

The information produced in an evaluation study is likely to be a source of power. This will certainly be the case where the primary purpose of evaluation is that of control, for example, central evaluation of decentralized training, or management commissioned evaluation. Most evaluative data should be useful rather than threatening, but training can never be evaluated without some judgements being made about the trainers responsible. This could account for the widespread defensiveness among practitioners when faced with proposals for evaluation. We have argued above that there are benefits in increasing the quality of the training and thus the effectiveness of the training department. Evaluation can also improve the relationship between the training department and the rest of the organization by producing evidence of real worth to the organization, by linking training events to improved organizational effectiveness, and by changing the relationship with line managers.

It is also necessary to recognize the political nature of evaluations. Organizations are usually comprised of groups of people with rather

---

Perhaps we might finish by asking you to draw up an action plan. Why not select something to evaluate? Aspects which need to be considered will include:

1 The cost of evaluating versus the likely benefits to:
   (a) the development of trainers
   (b) the improvement of the programme
   (c) future trainees
   (d) the relationship with line managers
2 The potential value of the evaluation data.
3 The likely impact of the programme on organizational goals and targets.
4 The resources available to conduct evaluation.
5 What data needs to be collected, how will it be collected, by whom?
6 The time frame for the evaluation.
7 Who is to receive the report and what process will be used?

For each stage of the proposed evaluation set a time for completion and try to analyse what (or who) is likely to hinder the achievement of that stage. It is also worth considering what you can do to mobilize support to overcome these possible hurdles.

different interests whose views on the importance of training and development will vary. Their opinions are often based upon information which is passing informally around the organizational networks. Formal evaluative data can challenge their opinions if this is thought necessary.

The very essence of evaluation in the way that we have described it in this book is to change the questions which people ask. As we said in the Introduction, changing the questions which people ask changes the way they think. We hope that by ending with a plan of action we have achieved what we were aiming for; that this is a book which not only looks at the theoretical aspects of evaluating training effectiveness but which offers a framework for practitioners to translate theory into practice.

Appendix 1
Analysing test scores

Item analysis

Testing is always time consuming. It is important to be sure that the time spent is effectively used. One method of avoiding time wasting is to eliminate ineffective test items.

- Each item in the test should be directly related to a training objective.
- Each item should be of proven worth, i.e. tested and found acceptable before it is used.
- Each item found effective should be 'banked' for later use.

Facility

The facility value (FV) is calculated in order to answer the question, 'how easy/difficult is the item?'. FV is the proportion of candidates who answered the item correctly.

Example: A questions with four alternative responses is set to 36 trainees. The following results are obtained:

Response	A	B	C	D	Total
Totals	17	10	5	4	36

(a) The correct response is B

(b) $FV = \dfrac{10}{36} = 0.28$

   (Note: Facility values should be calculated correct to two decimal places.)

(c) The facility value is very low; most have the wrong answer. Consider picking out the answer with a pin. One would expect 1 in 4 to be correct, i.e. $FV = 0.25$. The item is thus too difficult for the trainees and three questions should be asked (see Figure A1.1).

There is no clear answer to the question, 'What range of facility values is acceptable?'.

(a) If we are expecting trainers to achieve objectives we need facility values of 0.70 or higher. If more than 30 per cent are answering the item incorrectly something is wrong.

(b) If we want to discriminate between candidates, the best range is from 0.30 to 0.70.

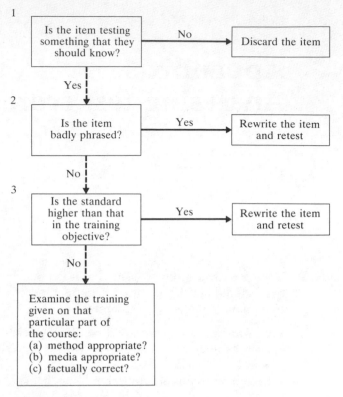

Figure A1.1   *Item analysis*

Discrimination

If a test item is playing its part, the good student will tend to get it correct and the poor student will tend to get it wrong. This tendency can be given a value—*the index of discrimination*—which falls between −1 and +1.

The *discrimination index (ID)* is usually calculated from the proportion of the top 27 per cent who answered correctly minus the proportion correct in the bottom 27 per cent. To take the example above of 36 answers to an item:

(a) 27% of 36 is approximately 10

$$\frac{36 \times 27}{100} = 9.72$$

(b) The group is then split into top 10 on the test as a whole, the bottom 10 and a middle group (see Table A1.1).

(c) The proportions correct are now calculated:

    (i)   top 27%   4 correct out of 10

$$\frac{4}{10} = 0.40$$

    (ii) bottom 27% 2 correct out of 10

$$\frac{2}{10} = 0.20$$

(d) The *ID* is then given by:

$$ID = 0.40 - 0.20$$
$$= 0.20$$

Table A1.1   *Calculating the index of discrimination*

Response	A	B*	C	D	Total
Top 10 on whole test	3	4	2	1	10
Middle 16	9	4	2	1	16
Bottom 10 on whole test	5	2	1	2	10
Totals	17	10	5	4	36

(B* is the correct response)

(e) This is a low *ID*. The top group show little more understanding than the bottom group and this is clearly unsatisfactory.

The figure of 27 per cent has been chosen as it gives the optimal size groups for discriminating, allowing for (1) maximizing the index and (2) using as much information as is possible given the constraint of (1). A reference for this is Kelley (1939).

The *ID* should never be negative—this would mean that the poorer trainees were more likely to get it correct. It cannot, however, be high with items which have high facility values—almost all the group will have answered the item correctly and there will be very little difference between the proportions.

Table A1.2 *Minimum values for ID*

FV	ID (min)
0.9	0.1
0.8	0.2
0.7	0.3
0.6	0.4
0.5	0.5
0.4	0.4
0.3	0.3

The minimum values for the *ID* recommended for differing facility bands are given in Table A1.2. If the *ID* falls below these values the item is faulty and needs rewriting.

Distractors   When using multichoice questions it is useful to examine the incorrect responses also. To take the 36 trainees tested on the 4 response choice item in Table A1.1:

(a) The distractor A has attracted almost half of the group. This is probably the key to the low facility value for the item. Either the instruction has misled them or the item is badly constructed, i.e. the phraseology of A is such that it seems correct to many students.

(b) The distractors C and D are both useful, attracting a few of the group. C has a positive index of discrimination but with such small numbers this is probably meaningless. With larger numbers this would be a cause for worry as it means that good students are more likely to pick this distractor.

Item banking It is wasteful not to keep for later use items which have acceptable *FV*s and *ID*s. They can be kept in an item bank on a card with a format like that in Figure A1.2. The question is written on the front and the rest of the information, in pencil, on the back.

Training objective

No .... Item No ....

	A	B*	C	D	Total
Top 27%					
Middle					
Bottom 27%					
Totals					

FV = ... *ID* = ...

Given to Course no ··· ··· ··· ··· ··· ··· ··· ··· ···

Note: B is given a * to show that that is the correct answer.

Figure A1.2 *Item banking card*

Comparing groups Sometimes we wish to compare two sets of scores to discover whether two courses produce the same results or if one course is superior.

Suppose Course A is trained on a CBL package while Course B follows the traditional course. The courses were matched for age, sex and pre-test knowledge. Their results on the post-test are:

				Students				
Course A	A_1	A_2	A_3	A_4	A_5	A_6	A_7	Mean
	82	78	79	92	77	72	87	81
Course B	B_1	B_2	B_3	B_4	B_5	B_6	B_7	Mean
	80	86	65	73	64	80	63	73

The simplest method of finding out is by visual inspection. Plot the scores on a base-line.

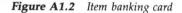

		B		
BBB	AB	AAABA	BA	A
60	70	80	90	100 marks

There is some overlap between the two groups. If there was no overlap group A would obviously be superior, e.g.

	BBBB	BB	B AAA	A	AAA
	60	70	80	90	100 marks

If the scores were completely mixed there would be no difference between groups, e.g.

	BAB	ABAB	A	B A B A B A
	60	70	80	90	100 marks

What we need as the basis for our decision is some measure of the amount of overlap—a large overlap means no difference, a small overlap means some difference. The method used was devised by Wilcoxon and developed by Mann-Whitney.

Table A1.3   *Critical values of U (p $\leqslant$ 0.05)*

n_1 is the smaller of the two groups

n_1 / n_2	2	3	4	5	6	7	8	9	10	11	12	13	14	15	16	17	18	19	20
3																			
4			0																
5		0	1	2															
6		1	2	4	5														
7		1	3	5	7	9													
8	0	2	4	6	8	10	13												
9	0	2	4	7	10	12	15	17											
10	0	3	5	8	11	14	17	20	23										
11	0	3	6	9	13	16	19	23	26	30									
12	1	4	7	11	14	18	22	26	29	33	37								
13	1	4	8	12	16	20	24	28	33	37	41	45							
14	1	5	9	13	17	22	26	31	36	40	45	50	55						
15	1	5	10	14	19	24	29	34	39	44	49	54	59	64					
16	1	6	11	15	21	26	31	37	42	47	53	59	64	70	75				
17	2	6	11	17	22	28	34	39	45	51	57	63	67	75	81	87			
18	2	7	12	18	24	30	36	42	48	55	61	67	74	80	86	93	99		
19	2	7	13	19	25	32	38	45	52	58	65	72	78	85	92	99	106	113	
20	2	8	13	20	27	34	41	48	55	62	69	76	83	90	98	105	112	119	127

If the figure calculated for U is *equal* to or *less* than that given in the body of the table, the groups are different. If the figure calculated for U is greater than that given in the table, the groups are not (statistically) different.

(a) Look at the plots in the first example on page 113 and calculate the number of times an A comes before a B. Start from the left.
   (i) There are no A plots before (i.e. lower than) the first 3 Bs
      U = 0 + 0 + 0
   (ii) There is one A plot before the fourth B
      U = 0 + 0 + 0 + 1

(iii) There are 4 A plots before the fifth and sixth Bs
$$U = 0 + 0 + 0 + 1 + 4 + 4$$
(iv) There are 5 A plots before the seventh B
$$U = 0 + 0 + 0 + 1 + 4 + 4 + 5$$

(b) The amount of overlap (U) is thus:
$$U = 14$$

(c) The size of the overlap depends upon the number of people involved. Here $n_1 = n_2 = 7$

(d) The critical value for U given in Table A1.3 for
$n_1 = n_2 = 7$ is 9

(e) The value which we have calculated (14) is greater than 9. Therefore, the groups are not statistically different.

The decision criterion used in constructing Table A1.3 is the prob-ability value 20 to 1 (0.05).

Reliability

People responsible for assessing trainees should keep it in mind that tests are are best imperfect measuring instruments of trainees' abilities or performance. Throughout all phases of the setting, administering and marking of tests the emphasis should be on ways and means of increasing the reliability of test scores.

An essential quality of any measuring instrument is that of reliability. In other words, reliable or consistent results ought to emerge from its use. In the assessment situation, there is little point in using a device which may fluctuate or vary with time. Ideally, one would hope that a test, for instance, when administered to two groups of very similar standards, would yield very similar results or, when administered to the same group subsequently, would produce very similar results.

Causes of low reliability

If an examiner sets and scores two different tests in the same subject, the trainees being tested are likely to obtain different scores on the two occasions.

Also, scores obtained by individual trainees in the same test are likely to show discrepancies when it is assessed by two examiners.

The main cause of poor reliability are:

(a) Changes in mental and physical states of the trainees which affect performance.
(b) Inconsistencies in the standards of scoring adopted by different examiners or by the same examiner on different occasions.
(c) Errors in scoring.
(d) Errors due to guessing.
(e) Incomplete sampling of the trainees' knowledge.

Absolute reliability will not be achieved. What is sought, therefore, is a reasonable level of reliability.

Reliability will be improved by:

(a) Increasing the length of the test—taking a larger, more adequate sample of training objectives.

(b) Maintaining standardized physical conditions, instructions, and so forth.

(c) Ensuring instructions are clear and unambiguous.

(d) Ensuring objective scoring by 'trained observers' or specialists or the use of marking guides for objective testing of knowledge.

Estimating the reliability of the scores

Test reliability can be assessed in two ways:

(a) Test a group of trainees twice and compare the results—test/retest.

(b) Compare the results on one half of the test with those on the other half—split-half.

Test/retest reliability

If a test is reliable one would expect a trainee, who scored a high mark on it today, to score a high mark on it again. Similarly people who score poor marks on the test could be expected to score poor marks on a second attempt. In other words, the test score on the 'test' should predict the score on the 'retest'.

Example: 10 trainees were tested and later retested on the same test. Their scores were:

Trainee	A	B	C	D	E	F	G	H	J	K
Test	11	8	4	4	7	2	10	7	4	3
Retest	10	7	5	2	6	2	9	5	3	3

These scores can be plotted on a scattergram (see Figure A1.3).

Test

	0	1	2	3	4	5	6	7	8	9	10	11	12
12													
11											A		
10										G			
9													
8							B						
7						H	E						
6													
5													
4			D	J		C							
3				K									
2			F										
1													
0													

Retest: 0 1 2 3 4 5 6 7 8 9 10 11 12

Retest

This sort of 'cigar shape' implies quite high reliability. The area at the bottom, where 4 can predict 2,3 or 5 detracts from perfect reliability.

Figure A1.3 (a) *Scattergram showing high reliability*

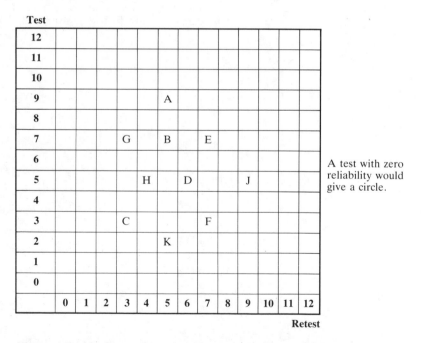

Figure A1.3(b) *Scattergram showing perfect reliability*

Figure A1.3(c) *Scattergram showing zero reliability*

Between the extremes of perfect reliability and no reliability is a grey area and, in order to make decisions about whether the test is reliable enough, we need to calculate a correlation coefficient between the two sets of scores.

Calculating a correlation coefficient

First plot the scattergram of the two sets of scores in Table A1.4 (see Figure A1.4).

Table A1.4 *Calculating the correlation coefficient*

Candidate	Test Score	
	Test X	**Test Y**
A	92	88
B	81	79
C	57	55
D	80	78
E	73	76
F	68	76
G	80	79
H	69	65
J	61	67
K	60	53

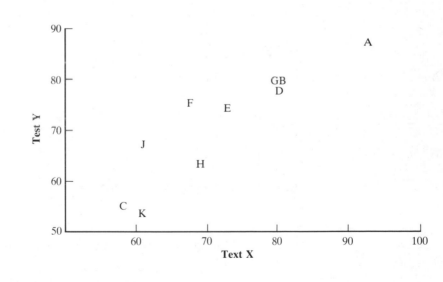

Figure A1.4 *Scattergram showing scores from Tests X and Y*

Now calculate the means and draw these as a cross on the scattergram (see Figure A1.5).

$$\Sigma x = 721 \quad \Sigma y = 716$$
$$\bar{x} = 72.1 \quad \bar{y} = 71.6$$

Count the number of people in each of the four quadrants of Figure A1.6.

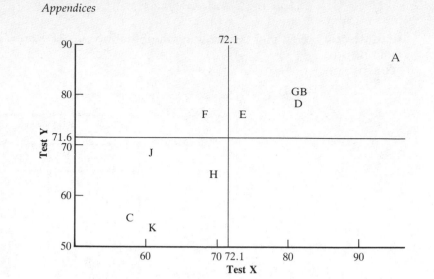

Figure A1.5 *Scattergram showing means of scores from Tests X and Y*

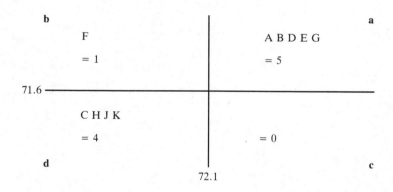

Figure A1.6 *Number of people in quadrants of the scattergram*

Cross multiply the number of scores in opposite quadrants:

$$ad = 5 \times 4 = 20$$
$$bc = 1 \times 1^* = 1$$
$$Q = \frac{ad}{bc} = 20$$
$$r = 0.84$$

* Note: a single empty quadrant is given the value 1.

Consult Table A1.5 of various values for ad/bc.

Table A1.5 *Pearson's Qs estimates of r_{tet} for various values of ad/bc*

ad/bc	r_{tet}	ad/bc	r_{tet}	ad/bc	r_{tet}
0–1.00	0.00	2.49–2.55	0.35	8.50–8.90	0.70
1.01–1.03	0.01	2.56–2.63	0.36	8.91–9.35	0.71
1.04–1.06	0.02	2.64–2.71	0.37	9.36–9.82	0.72
1.07–1.08	0.03	2.72–2.79	0.38	9.83–10.33	0.73
1.09–1.11	0.04	2.80–2.87	0.39	10.34–10.90	0.74
1.12–1.14	0.05	2.88–2.96	0.40	10.91–11.51	0.75
1.15–1.17	0.06	2.97–3.05	0.41	11.52–12.16	0.76
1.18–1.20	0.07	3.06–3.14	0.42	12.17–12.89	0.77
1.21–1.23	0.08	3.15–3.24	0.43	12.90–13.70	0.78
1.24–1.27	0.09	3.25–3.34	0.44	13.71–14.58	0.79
1.28–1.30	0.10	3.35–3.45	0.45	14.59–15.57	0.80
1.31–1.33	0.11	3.46–3.56	0.46	15.58–16.65	0.81
1.34–1.37	0.12	3.57–3.68	0.47	16.66–17.88	0.82
1.38–1.40	0.13	3.69–3.80	0.48	17.89–19.28	0.83
1.41–1.44	0.14	3.81–3.92	0.49	19.29–20.85	0.84
1.45–1.48	0.15	3.93–4.06	0.50	20.86–22.68	0.85
1.49–1.52	0.16	4.07–4.20	0.51	22.69–24.76	0.86
1.53–1.56	0.17	4.21–4.34	0.52	24.77–27.22	0.87
1.57–1.60	0.18	4.35–4.49	0.53	27.23–30.09	0.88
1.61–1.64	0.19	4.50–4.66	0.54	30.10–33.60	0.89
1.65–1.69	0.20	4.67–4.82	0.55	33.61–37.79	0.90
1.70–1.73	0.21	4.83–4.99	0.56	37.80–43.06	0.91
1.74–1.78	0.22	5.00–5.18	0.57	43.07–49.83	0.92
1.79–1.83	0.23	5.19–5.38	0.58	49.84–58.79	0.93
1.84–1.88	0.24	5.39–5.59	0.59	58.80–70.95	0.94
1.89–1.93	0.25	5.60–5.80	0.60	70.96–89.01	0.95
1.94–1.98	0.26	5.81–6.03	0.61	89.02–117.54	0.96
1.99–2.04	0.27	6.04–6.28	0.62	117.55–169.67	0.97
2.05–2.10	0.28	6.29–6.54	0.63	169.68–293.12	0.98
2.11–2.15	0.29	6.55–6.81	0.64	293.13–923.97	0.99
2.16–2.22	0.30	6.82–7.10	0.65	923.98–	1.00
2.23–2.28	0.31	7.11–7.42	0.66		
2.29–2.34	0.32	7.43–7.75	0.67		
2.35–2.41	0.33	7.76–8.11	0.68		
2.42–2.48	0.34	8.12–8.49	0.69		

Compute $\dfrac{bc}{ad}$ if it is larger than $\dfrac{ad}{bc}$

b	a
d	c

r will then be negative

The *reliability coefficient* is an important piece of information. Tests with law coefficients do not accurately grade students. In the table below students have been graded A – E on their test results. As the reliability coefficient decreases so the proportion awarded an incorrect grade increases.

$$r = 1.00 \qquad \text{Incorrectly graded} = \quad 0\%$$

0.9	23%
0.8	33%
0.7	40%
0.5	50%

Decisions based upon a trainee's grades where the reliability of the test is less than 0.8 are suspect.

Split-half reliability   It is rarely possible to test and retest trainees. An alternative is to split the test into two halves—usually odd items and even items—then correlate the two halves as if they were two tests, as above.

Example: 10 trainees take a test with 40 items in it. The test is marked and the results split as below:

Candidate	Number of odd items correct (X)	Number of even items correct (Y)
A	15	12
B	19	16
C	16	17
D	18	18
E	17	20
F	16	15
G	15	10
H	14	13
J	16	14
K	19	19

Plot the candidates on a scattergram and work out the means (see Figure A1.7).

b   C   B D E K   a

  = 1   = 4
                                                    $Q = \dfrac{a\,d}{b\,c}$

15.4 ─────────────┼─────────────────
                                                    $= \dfrac{20}{1}$

    A F G H J

    = 5   = 0 $r = \underline{0.84}$

d   c
            16.5

Figure A1.7   *Scattergram of scores showing split-half reliability*

Appendix 2
Designing questionnaires and analysing the data

Most of the information used by evaluators is gathered by the use of structured interviews and questionnaires. There is a good deal of similarity between the two methods and the two techniques can often be combined with the evaluator administering a questionnaire on the more quantitative aspects, then following this up with an interview.

Questionnaires are used more frequently than interviews; this is due to a combination of some of the following advantages:

- Questionnaires are much cheaper; it is expensive to have interviewers travelling long distances and interviewing large numbers of people.
- Much larger samples can be taken using questionnaires and the questions can be administered to a large sample simultaneously.
- By careful design, the processing of questionnaire answers can be made very simple and efficient.
- It is often easier to convince respondents of the anonymity of their answers if they are filling in a questionnaire as opposed to undergoing a face to face interview.

On the other hand, questionnaires have a number of disadvantages when compared with interviews. These stem primarily from the greater flexibility within the interview situation, where the evaluator can follow leads as necessary and is not confined to the printed questions. Questionnaires are also likely to elicit response biases as respondents have a tendency to answer the questions in what they perceive to be a socially acceptable manner.

Planning the questionnaire

The most important stage in the use of a questionnaire is the planning before it is drafted. The following questions need to be answered:

- Is a questionnaire the best method of collecting the data?
- What information is required?
- Who is to provide this information?
- What type of analysis will be carried out on the information collected?

All of these questions are, of course, interlinked and decisions taken on one question may well determine the answer to other questions.

The type of information required will often determine the format of the questionnaire and this will control the analysis of the data collected. It is therefore necessary to think about this before the design stage.

The ideal sample consists of everyone who has relevant information and one of the advantages of a questionnaire approach is that this is sometimes possible. If the numbers involved are less than 200, this is probably the best strategy. If very large numbers are involved or the resources available to collect and analyse the data are limited, it may be necessary to select a sample from the total population (i.e. everyone who is of interest). If the sample is carefully drawn, it should be possible to use the data as representative of that which would have been collected had the whole population responded.

A simple random sample of respondents can be selected by procedures such as drawing numbers from a hat, taking names at regular intervals from an alphabetical list, or using tables of random numbers. If the variation of opinions within the total population is not thought to be great, a simple random sample of 20 per cent to 30 per cent should give representative information.

If it is thought likely that there will be wide variations in the opinion held by people in different parts of the organization or in different organizations, then a stratified sample may give a better estimate. In this, the total population is broken down into major divisions or strata, and a random sample is taken from each stratum. For instance, in following up a junior management programme, the strata could be the functions in which the people now work. Some strata will have more people in them and need a bigger sample; some will have more variation in them and again need a bigger sample.

A questionnaire can be completed either with or without supervision. The method of administration will affect the design and must be taken into account during the planning stage. Unsupervised questionnaires need very careful design and pilot runs will be necessary to eliminate ambiguities. They must also be simple. Supervised questionnaires can be more complex.

Closed questions, where the respondent is asked to select one answer from a number of alternatives, are easy to analyse and the questionnaire can be designed so that the analysis may be carried out mechanically. If the sample is large and a number of issues are to be investigated then most of the questions should be of this type. Open-ended questions, where respondents are allowed to write in whatever they please, are very difficult to analyse. It will be necessary to establish categories so that the information can be summarized in a usable form, and this will involve a good deal of time. This must be clearly understood and anticipated at the planning stage. Open questions allow people the opportunity to express their particular point of view rather than being confined to pre-determined answers. This makes some people feel more at ease. The choice of format for the questions should be governed by the sort of information required, the ease with which useful information can be extracted from the responses, and *convenience for the respondents*. The co-operation of the respondents is essential; long and complicated questionnaires will only antagonize them. It is important to try to make them 'user-friendly'.

Questionnaire construction

To ensure willing co-operation, the purpose of the questionnaire must be explained either in a written introduction or by the person administering it. Instructions on how to complete it should be simple and clear. Above all, the document should give the impression that it has been carefully prepared and produced.

Answers to early questions tend to be unreliable, so it is best to start with something factual like personal details. If response becomes mechanical, the answers again become inaccurate. It is therefore worth thinking about different sections to the document, each with a different layout.

All questions should be written in a way which helps those who are answering them to do so accurately. The questions should therefore be as short as possible and be phrased in language which the respondents will understand. The intention is not to confuse them with complicated constructions; even the use of negatives, as in the first part of this sentence, will confuse some.

Closed questions will often take up a large part of the questionnaire as they are easier for the respondent to answer and for the evaluator to analyse. The simplest form is a binary question like:

In your present job is it necessary for you to:

Diagnose mechanical faults in	Yes/No
Repair	Yes/No
Supervise someone using	Yes/No

Where there are a number of possible answers, a polylog question can be used:

To what extent are you involved in writing proposals for..............................?

- ☐ I write them
- ☐ I advise on them
- ☐ I make some recommendations
- ☐ I am not involved

Sometimes preference scales are used to assess the strength of attitudes. There are several formats for this. The best offer two opposite statements and a space for responses.

I find my work very interesting	1	2	3	4	5	6	7	I find my work deadly dull

The response space can be labelled rather than numbered.

Statement X	Strongly agree X	Agree X	Neutral	Agree Y	Strongly agree Y	Statement Y
The interviewer seemed very interested in me as a person						The interviewer didn't seem to be at all interested in me as a person

When it is difficult to produce opposites an agree/disagree format can be used:

Statement	Strongly agree	Agree	Undecided	Disagree	Strongly disagree
I feel that . . .					
. . . is an important objective of my job					

Open-ended questions can often be included at the pilot stage and later converted into questions which are easier to analyse. The range of responses which are offered can be content analysed and the themes then used as categories for closed questions. For example, in the pilot we might ask, 'What topics which would be useful to you in your job, were not covered on the course?'. The question which would then be included in the questionnaire proper might be:

The following have been recommended as areas where extensions to the basic course would be helpful:

Technique	Do you agree?		If yes, what particularly?
	yes	no	
Network analysis			
Costing			
etc.			

The question would usually be followed by an open-ended one:

Are there other topics which you think should be included?

Topic . . .   What would you have found particularly useful?

The value in this sort of approach is that it increases the response rate. Most people will answer 'yes' or 'no' if asked, 'Do you think that X would have been useful to you?'. Not many people answer questions of the type, 'What do you think ought to be done?'.

The construction of the questionnaire is not complete until it has been tried on a sample of the target population and shown to give the sorts of answers which were expected. Respondents often do not interpret questions in the same way as the writer and the only way to sort out ambiguities is to ask the questions and discuss the answers. The best way to carry out the pilot is to sit with a few of the respondents and encourage them to discuss questions which are difficult to understand or to answer.

Distribution of questionnaires

Postal distribution is the most popular method but contacting the respondents personally or through an agent is likely to produce a better response rate. As well as the questionnaire itself, there will usually be a covering letter. This should explain the purpose of the investigation and thank the respondent for the time spent in answering the questions. If there is an official sponsor of the project this should also be stated. The date by which the questionnaire is to be returned should be stated. Don't give respondents more than three weeks or they will put it to one side and forget it. If the form is to be returned by post, a stamped addressed envelope should be provided.

The intention is to get as high a response rate as possible. When less than 70 per cent of the questionnaires are returned, there must be grave doubts about whether the responses are representative. Random sampling is not achieved by low response rates.

Analysis of data

The simplest method of summarizing questionnaire data is some form of frequency statement. For example:

	Strongly agree X	Agree X	Undecided	Agree Y	Strongly agree Y	
Statement X	3	25	10	10	2	Statement Y

This represents the distribution of the opinions of 50 people on the statements X and Y.

A refinement would be to express the numbers in the boxes as percentages of the total number surveyed. In our example this would become:

	SA X	A X	Un	A Y	SA Y	
X	6%	50%	20%	20%	4%	Y

This is easier to understand when the number of people surveyed is not a round number. Percentages can be misleading if small numbers are involved. The total number surveyed should appear somewhere in the summary. It is, of course, easy to show frequencies or percentages as bar graphs if it is felt that this is likely to increase understanding.

Sometimes the opinions are reduced to a mean response for the purpose of comparisons. The boxes are given numbers and the frequencies multiplied by these. For instance, in the example above:

	1	2	3	4	5	
X	3	25	10	10	2	Y
Weight =	3	+ 50	+ 30	+ 40	+ 10	
=	133					
Average =	2.7					

Appendices

This is a very dubious exercise. There is no reason to believe that the intervals between the boxes are equal and there is therefore no justification for using processes of multiplication or division.

If it is intended to compare one set of opinions with another, the correct method is to use the chi-squared statistic rather than the mean response. Suppose that we have two sets of opinions extracted from two courses about a particular issue.

Statement X	Agree X	Tend to agree X	Undecided	Tend to agree Y	Agree Y	Statement Y
Course A	10	20	10	5	5	
Course B	5	10	15	5	5	

If the proportions across the boxes are similar then there is no statistical difference between the frequencies. In this case we could estimate the frequency in any one box from the frequencies in the others and produce a figure that is quite close to the one actually found.

Estimating the frequencies in the boxes and comparing these with the actual frequencies found is the basis of the chi-squared test. Where large differences are found, the frequencies can be said to represent different opinions, or pass rates or whatever.

To take the example above. First of all find the row and column totals

	X	N		Y		Totals
Course A	10	20	10	5	5	50
Course B	5	10	25	5	5	50
Totals	15	30	35	10	10	100

Now calculate the 'expected value' in each cell from the formula:

$$\frac{\text{Row total} \times \text{Column total}}{\text{Overall total}}$$

For the first cell this is
$$\frac{50 \times 15}{100} = 7.5$$

For the second
$$\frac{50 \times 30}{100} = 15$$

For the third
$$\frac{50 \times 35}{100} = 17.5$$

Fill in the new block by writing the expected values in brackets underneath the actual, observed values.

10	20	10	5	5	50
(7.5)	(15)	(17.5)	(5)	(5)	
5	10	25	5	5	50
(7.5)	(15)	(17.5)	(5)	(5)	
15	30	35	10	10	100

Subtract all the expected values from the observed values and calculate chi-squared from the formula

$$\chi^2 = \sum \frac{(\text{Observed}-\text{Expected})^2}{\text{Expected}}$$

i.e. $\chi^2 = \dfrac{(10-7.5)^2}{7.5} + \dfrac{(20-15)^2}{15} + \dfrac{(10-17.5)^2}{17.5}$

$$+ \frac{(5-5)^2}{5} + \frac{(5-5)^2}{5} + \frac{(5-7.5)^2}{7.5} + \frac{(10-15)^2}{15}$$

$$+ \frac{(25-17.5)^2}{17.5} + \frac{(5-5)^2}{5} + \frac{(5-5)^2}{5}$$

$$= 0.833 + 1.667 + 3.21 + 0 + 0 + 0.833 + 1.667 + 3.21 + 0 + 0$$

$$\chi^2 = 11.42$$

The figure of 11.42 is a measure of the difference in the opinions expressed by the two courses. We must now decide whether it is large enough to discount chance variation and state what the opinions are.

The table of critical values (Table A2.1) is based on the 1 in 20 criterion. The degrees of freedom are calculated from:

df = (Number of rows − 1) (Number of columns −1)

In this case we have

df = (2 − 1) (5 − 1) = 4

The critical value for df 4 is 9.49. The figure for χ^2 that we have calculated (11.42) is larger than this thus can we say that the expressed opinions of the two groups are different.

df = (r−1)(c−1)	Critical values for χ²	df = (r−1)(c−1)	Critical values for χ²
1	3.84	20	31.41
2	5.99	21	32.67
3	7.81	22	33.92
4	9.49	23	35.17
5	11.07	24	36.42
6	12.59	25	37.65
7	14.07	26	38.89
8	15.51	27	40.11
9	16.92	28	41.34
10	18.31	29	42.56
11	19.68	30	43.77
12	21.03	40	55.76
13	22.36	50	67.50
14	23.68	60	79.08
15	25.00	70	90.53
16	26.30	80	101.9
17	27.59	90	113.1
18	28.87	100	124.3
19	30.14		

Table A2.1 *Critical values for χ^2 ($p \leqslant 0.05$)*

The value for χ^2 is computed from

$$\chi^2 = \sum \frac{(O - E)^2}{E}$$

Appendix 3 Designing interviews and analysing the data

The interview is a widely used technique for gathering evaluation data. The interviewer can ask direct questions, and further probing and clarification is possible as the interview proceeds. This flexibility is very valuable for exploring issues as it can give more depth to the investigation than is possible when using questionnaires.

Interviews may be highly structured, resembling questionnaires, but usually start with general questions to allow the respondent to talk about some of the issues which he or she feels are important. Sometimes interviews will be exploratory and will have very little pre-planned structure. An example would be the rather informal discussions of 'how things are going' which take place in the bar on residential courses.

Interviewing typically involves a one-to-one interaction but it can be carried out with a group. Group interviews save time and allow the respondents to build on each other's responses, but this influence sometimes leads the group in a direction which none of the individuals would have chosen. The situation may also inhibit the contribution of group members as some people are inclined not to express views if they feel that they are in a minority. The empathic relationship which is the hallmark of a good interview is more difficult to achieve in a group setting. There is also the problem of the situation giving undue prominence to the statements of those who are more articulate or more confident.

Planning

The first decision to be made by the evaluator is whether interviewing is the most appropriate method of data collection. It will be particularly useful when: re-appraising previously identified training needs; exploring the extent of transfer of learning; examining the effectiveness of particular training methods; and, when trying to relate activities to organizational goals and purposes.

A major drawback of interviews is the time taken to conduct and analyse them. As we found with questionnaires, personal bias can distort the data. With interviews this is not only self-report bias, but also the bias of the interviewer. The type of question asked and the nature of the interaction will encourage certain kinds of responses and discourage others. Interviewing takes considerable skill if valid data is to be collected. Interviewers must understand their own biases and those of the respondents. They must also be able to listen actively and to change the shape of the interview in order to probe issues which arise. If the respondents are to raise sensitive issues and offer frank statements, it will also be necessary to establish an empathic relationship with the respondents.

The next step in planning is to decide what information is sought and thus what questions must be asked. A rough interview schedule is drafted and tested on a colleague. It is then refined and piloted with a few members of the target population. The schedule will help the interviewer by providing a reminder of the points to be explored. It should not be so detailed that it dictates the whole pattern of the interview. Interviewing should be a flexible process which allows the exploration of themes which were not anticipated when the schedule was drawn up. If it has a rigid format, the data can be more economically collected by using a questionnaire.

Questions for the schedule could include some of the following:

Questions	**Probing**
What did you hope to get out of the course before you went on it?	To find out if expectations were realistic.
Did it meet with your expectations?	If not, why not?
What were the most useful things that you learned?	Useful for job performance? In what way useful?
What are you doing differently since the programme?	Ask for specific examples; try to connect to learning.
• anything else?	Describe a specific incident.
Did you talk to your supervisor when you returned?	What kind of debrief? What benefit from it?

Specific questions can be asked about particular aspects of the programme; ask what candidates thought were its strengths or weaknesses; ask about aspects which were new or had been tried for the first time, etc:

Is there anything else that you would like to say about the programme?

Is there anything that we haven't talked about that you think we should have talked about?

Contracting Establishing a good relationship with the interviewee is the purpose of the early part of the interview. What should happen is that a form of contract is negotiated. The interviewee will have questions (although these may not be asked) and the answers to them will form the basis of the contract. Areas which should be discussed will include:

- Who am I? Why am I here? What are my goals?
- Who am I working for?
- What do I want from you and what am I going to do with the information?
- Who will see the data and in what format will it then be?
- How will I protect your confidentiality?

There is a further question about whether the interviewee believes that the investigator can be trusted. A powerful aid to building a trusting relationship is for the interviewer to provide short factual summaries during the interview. The interviewee can then be assured that the interviewer is at least listening to what is being said and has understood it. It is, of course, also possible for the interviewee to correct any misunderstanding and thus become an active participant in the recording of the data.

Data gathering

The interview will often fall into two parts: an initial exploratory phase of rather general discussion, and a second phase during which specific issues are pursued. This order is recommended as it makes it more likely that the interviewee will raise issues rather than being confined only to the areas which he or she thinks that the interviewer is interested in.

Recording information with a highly structured interview is a simple process of making short notes in the spaces left on the schedule. Less structured interviews pose more difficult problems. Taking notes is the most common method and, with practice, this will record most of the useful information. Key words, phrases and quotes are recorded during the interview and these are expanded before the next interview can interfere with the memory. Taking detailed notes during the interview will interfere with the flow and with the rapport. Few interviewees enjoy talking to the top of someone's head.

It is possible to use a tape recorder; this has the advantage of providing a complete record of the interview. However, this procedure will inhibit some interviewees. Many people are wary of making statements on sensitive issues when these can be played back verbatim somewhere else. A further disadvantage of this method is the length of time taken to access the information. For an interview lasting one hour, it will take about two hours to extract the main points from the recording and about four hours to make a complete transcription.

While carrying out the interview, the sensitive interviewer will realize the importance of his or her own behaviour in controlling that of the interviewee. For instance, people who avoid eye contact and regularly avert their gaze when speaking are usually suspected of being 'economical with the truth'. However, such gaze aversion can easily be induced by an interviewer who sits too close to the interviewee. Similarly, people who make false starts to sentences and then rephrase what they were going to say, are often suspected of embroidering the story. Such behaviour can easily be induced by an interviewer who has too much eye contact and who is thus perceived to be an interrogator.

Talking is often seen as active and listening as being passive. However, effective listening is an active combination of hearing, checking understanding, clarifying contradictions and summarizing what has been said. It also requires some commitment to exploring the respondent's viewpoint in as unbiased a way as possible. We all have pre-conceived ideas based upon experience, personal values, expectations of other people and untested prejudices. All of these can filter and distort what is heard. The more aware the interviewer is of these elements, the better able he or she will be to control biases in what is recorded. Reflective summaries provide an opportunity to check and correct distortions of the messages being offered. Many programmes designed to train interviewers use video-recordings for feedback. This is one area where such feedback can be particularly valuable, allowing people to see for themselves just how biased they are.

Termination

Towards the end of the interview it is good practice to briefly restate some of the main themes and give the interviewee an opportunity to add additional comments. Some open-ended questions such as, 'Is there anything that you think I should have asked about, but haven't?', will sometimes uncover topics which have been overlooked. A little caution is in order here as some interviewees will take this opportunity to open floodgates. It may be worth while prefacing the question with, 'I'd like to use the last few minutes . . .'.

The interviewee should be allowed the opportunity to ask questions. There may, for instance, still be some doubts about the purpose of the interview or the level of confidentiality. The interview should be ended properly by expressing thanks. This carries through the good atmosphere in which the interview should have taken place and a statement of the respondent's contribution helps to create goodwill.

Data analysis

Interviews can yield large amounts of information and this will need summarizing. This can be done by extracting short quotations which are thought to be representative, or by writing a short passage which is a summary of the main themes which were discussed. More often, a number of interviews are summarized for a report which will have main themes. The summary then becomes a mixture of statistical statements and more qualitative information.

Forty-three of the 57 managers interviewed had not had a debriefing session with their supervisor on return from the programme. In the 14 cases where debriefing had occurred, the benefits were reported as being:

Creation of opportunities to use new skills (9 cases)
Negotiation of the possibilities for progressing the action plan (6 cases)
More open relationship with the supervisor (4 cases)
Opportunity to discuss further development (3 cases)

Direct quotations have great impact and sometimes will be the only part which the reader remembers. Therefore, they should be used sparingly and more often when they represent a widely held view. A well-turned phrase which represents the view of only one respondent may distort the understanding of the report.

Appendix 4   Observing as an evaluative technique

One of the most direct methods of collecting evaluative data is by observing people in their work setting. The observation may be unstructured, with the person who is observing being as open-minded as possible and using his or her judgement about which events are considered important. Alternatively it may be highly structured by the use of coded schedules which guide attention to specific types of event. The latter is more likely in evaluations of training. The categories which are selected will be those where changes are expected as a result of training, or those which are thought to be particularly important to the success of the job. In practice, the observer will often use both of these approaches, as an open-ended method can complement the rather narrow field observed with a highly structured one. Sometimes the observer will start with a relatively unstructured approach and later focus on aspects which seem to be of importance. This is the approach which Parlett and Hamilton (1977) have called 'progressive focusing'.

The recording of the information may be done during the observation or immediately after it. The former is better for detail and the latter for overall impressions. The longer the interval between the observation and the recording, the less accurate the information will be. If it is intended to quote actual statements these must be recorded faithfully and in quotation marks. There may be a case for using a tape recorder to ensure accuracy in such cases. Tape recorders may well introduce problems into the situation because those being observed are less likely to act naturally when they know that they are being recorded. People do get used to them and after a while, forget that they are there, but this may not happen in a short session.

Observations are free from the biases of self-reports in interviews or questionnaires because the evaluator is directly connected with behaviour rather than someone's perceptions of it. However, the evaluator must be sensitive to the situation and the likelihood that his or her presence will distort the performance being observed. Also the same hazards apply as in interviewing if the observer is biased and sees only what he or she expects or wants to see.

Observing interpersonal skills of individuals

If used correctly, observations can be particularly helpful in examining interpersonal skills and relationships with others. In observing the interactions of an individual with colleagues or customers, a set of categories like those developed by Rackham and Morgan (1977) can be used. The thirteen types of behaviour are listed on a sheet of paper and the frequency with which they are used in some significant period of time is recorded. Specific instances of appropriate or inappropriate use of a particular category are also recorded to be used as feedback. The categories are shown in Figure 7.2. After familiarization with the use of these, the observer could work with a sheet like Table A4.1.

Table A4.1 *Categories for observing individual interactions*

Behaviour	Frequency	Specific Incidents
Proposing		
Building		
Supporting		
Disagreeing		
Defending/attacking		
Blocking/difficulty stating		
Open behaviour		
Testing understanding		
Summarizing		
Seeking information		
Giving information		
Shutting out		
Bringing in		

Source: Rackham and Morgan 1977.

It is common experience that two people observing the same event will later give different accounts of it. Putting in a lot of structure by using a checklist like the one above, will control some of this, but it will still be necessary to practise in order to produce reliable observations.

Observing groups at work

Interpersonal relationships are a key component of working in groups and observing interactions within the group setting can provide useful information about the nature of those relationships.

Broad categories like the following will reveal many of the important aspects:

Interruptions
- Who interrupts the most, and the least?
- Who is interrupted the most, and the least?

Air space
- Who talks most, and who least?
- Who attempts to dominate the conversation?

Disagreement
- How often do they disagree?
- How do they settle disagreements?

Support
- How often do they support each other?
- Who supports whom?

If the purpose of the group is to make decisions, a checklist like Table A4.2 might be useful.

Table A4.2 Decision-making in groups

Who provided the structure?	Group member					
	A	B	C	D	E	F
• Follows the structure provided by others						
• Provided a plan for meeting goals which was discussed						
• Provided a plan for reaching decisions which was implemented						
How was information given?						
• Gave incorrect information or withheld something important						
• Gave information in a disorganized fashion						
• Gave information which was relevant and concise						
Who made the decisions?						
• Avoided making decisions, accepted others' decisions						
• Proposed solutions for others to approve (or disapprove)						
• Proposed the solutions which were implemented						
Investment of energy						
• Low—kept silent except when asked something						
• Moderate—active for much of the time						
• High—the most active group member						

Observing a training session

One important use of observation within an evaluative strategy is the observation of training sessions. This has three main phases: some discussion with the trainer before the session, the observation itself, and some feedback afterwards.

During the pre-observation discussion, the trainer is asked what he or she is trying to achieve, i.e. for aims and objectives. The trainer is then asked to describe the shape of the session and why the specific methods have been chosen. Some discussion should occur about how the observational record will be used, to what extent the information is confidential, and to whom. It is also good practice to ask the trainer if there are any specific aspects of the session on which he or she would like feedback.

During the session the observer should be as unobtrusive as possible. Sometimes observers become active participants in the session, but this can be difficult for the trainer and it will also make it very difficult for the observer to record information. Notes should be made during the session with some detail on specific incidents. Some framework will usually be necessary in order to classify incidents. One which we have found useful is shown in Table A4.3 (see p 138). Under 'further comments' the following questions might be addressed:

- To what extent did the methods seem suitable for *this* group?
- What form of assessment of trainee progress was being used?
- How was feedback given to the trainees?

The post-observation feedback should occur as soon as possible after the session. This should begin by asking the trainer what he or she thought of the actual session compared with that expected and planned. The observer should then discuss specific incidents and how they were seen by observer, trainees and trainer. This works best when incidents where things went well are discussed first. People are generally more inclined to accept the observer's opinion when discussion of positive events precedes that of incidents when things did not go well (Stone, Guertal and McIntosh, 1984). Whatever the purpose of the observation, the feedback is intended to be a helpful reflection for the trainer and it should not be heavily judgemental.

A video camera in the background can support observations. This has the advantage of full data which can later be observed by more than one person and thus be impartially classified. This is often useful for feedback during the training of interviewers, trainers, etc. as they can afterwards see how they appear to others. It may also be suitable for research and for training in observation skills. It is time consuming and may not be a cost-effective method of gathering evaluative data.

Appendices

Table A4.3 *Trainer appraisal form*

Name of trainer: .... Title of session: ....

Length: ....

Place a 'X' in the box if you feel that area needs improvement, and please elaborate with comments.

Signposting	X	Comments
Introduced subject		
Referred to objectives		
Indicated main stages		
Summarized to consolidate stages		
Explained procedures		
Use of aids		
Flip chart		
White board		
Over-head projector		
Computer demonstration		
Other		
Delivery technique		
Voice (volume, tone, pace)		
Listened		
Use of questions		
Group involvement		
Checked understanding		
Eye contact		
Mannerisms		
Control		
Allocated time well		
Maintained good pace		
Kept to subject		
Overall impression		
Knowledgeable		
Enthusiastic		
Aware of group needs		
Created interest		

Any further comments:

Observer: Date:

Bibliography

Bandura, A. (1977) *Social Learning Theory*, Prentice-Hall, Englewood Cliffs, N.J.

Bandura, A. (1986) *Social Foundations of Thought and Action*, Prentice-Hall, Englewood Cliffs, N.J.

Belbin, R.M. (1981) *Management Teams: Why they Succeed or Fail*, Heinemann, London.

Bennett, R. and T. Leduchowicz (1983) 'What makes for an effective trainer?', *Journal of European Industrial Training Monograph*, 7, 2.

Berger, M. (1977) 'Training and the organisational context', *Journal of European Industrial Training*, 1, 2, 7–12.

Blake, R.R. and J.S. Mouton (1964) *The Managerial Grid*, Gulf, Houston.

Blake, R.R. and J.S. Mouton (1969) *Building a Dynamic Corporation through Grid Organisation Development*, Addison-Wesley, Reading, Mass.

Bolt, J.F. (1987) 'Trends in management training and executive education', *Journal of Management Development*, 6, 5–15.

Burns, T. and G.M. Stalker (1961) *The Management of Innovation*, London, Tavistock.

Byham, W.C. (1982) 'How assessment centers are used to evaluate training effectiveness', *'Training'* (*The Magazine of Human Resource Development*), Feb.

Cameron, K. (1980) 'Critical questions in assessing organisational effectiveness', *Organisational Dynamics*, Autumn, 66–80.

Cascio, W.F. (1982) *Costing Human Resources: The Financial Impact of Behaviour in Organisations*, Kent, Boston.

Chapple, E.D. and L.R. Sayles (1961) *The Measurement of Managements*, Macmillan, New York.

Cook, J.D., S.J. Hepworth, T.D. Wall and P.B. Warr (1981) *The Experience of Work*, Academic Press, London.

Critchley, B. and D. Casey (1984) 'Second thoughts on team building', *Management Education and Development*, 15, 2, 163–175.

Cronbach, L.J. (1963) 'Course improvement through evaluation', *Teachers College Record*, 64, 672–683.

Dale, B.G. and T.S. Ball (1983) *A Study of Quality Circles in UK Manufacturing Organisations*, Dept of Management Sciences, UMIST, Manchester.

Dale, B.G. and S.G. Hayward (1984) 'Some reasons for quality circle failure', *Leadership and Organisational Development Journal*, Parts I, II and III.

Davies, I.K. (1971) *The Management of Learning*, McGraw-Hill, London.

Easterby-Smith, M. (1986) *Evaluation of Management Education, Training and Development*, Gower, Aldershot.

Faley, R.H. and E. Sandstrom (1985) 'Content representativeness: an empirical method of evaluation', *Journal of Applied Psychology*, 70, 567–571.

Ford, J.K. and S.P. Wroten (1984) 'Introducing new methods for conducting training evaluation and for linking training evaluation to program design', *Personnel Psychology*, 37, 651–656.

Gagné, R.M. (1970) *The Conditions of Learning*, Holt, Rinehart and Winston, New York.

Georgeopolous, B.S. and A.S. Tannenbaum (1957) 'The study of organisational effectiveness', *American Sociological Review*, 22, 534–540.

Glossary of Training Terms (1971) Department of Employment, HMSO.

Goldstein, A.P. and M. Sorcher (1974) *Changing Supervisor Behavior*, Pergammon Press, New York.

Goldstein, I.L. (1980) 'Training in work organisations', *Annual Review of Psychology*, 229–272.

Goldstein, I.L. (1986) *Training in Organisations*, 2nd edition, Brooks/Cole, California.

Goodman, P.S. and J.W. Dean (1982) 'Creating long-term organisational change', In Goodman and Associates, *Change in Organisations*, Jossey Bass, California.

Hagman, J. and A. Rose (1983) 'Retention of military tasks: a review', *Human Factors*, 25, 193–213.

Hamblin, A.C. (1974) *Evaluation and Control of Training*, McGraw-Hill, London.

Handy, C. (1981) *Understanding Organisations*, Penguin, Harmondsworth.

Havelock, R.G. (1969) *Planning for Innovation through Dissemination and Utilization of Knowledge*, Institute for Social Research, University of Michigan.

Hayes, R.H. (1981) 'Why Japanese factories work', *Harvard Business Review*, July/August, 57–62.

Henerson, M.E., L.L. Morris and C.T. Fitzgibbon (1978) *How to Measure Attitudes*, Sage, Beverly Hills.

Hinrichs, J.R. (1976) 'Personnel Training', Ch. 19 of M.D. Dunnette (Ed.) *Handbook of Organisational and Industrial Psychology*, Rand McNally, Chicago.

Hussey, D.E. (1985) 'Implementing Corporate Strategy: using management education and training', *Long Range Plan*, 18, 5, 28–37.

Ishikawa, K. (1968) *Quality Circles Activities*, Union of Japanese Scientists and Engineers, Tokyo, Japan.

Katz, D. and R.L. Khan (1978) *The Social Psychology of Organizations*, 2nd edition, Wiley, New York.

Kearsley, E. (1982) *Costs, Benefits and Productivity in Training Systems*, Addison-Wesley, Reading, Massachussetts.

Kelley (1939) 'The selection of upper and lower groups for the validation of test items', *Journal of Educational Psychology*, 30, 17–24.

Kirkpatrick, D.L. (1959) 'Techniques for evaluating training programmes', *Journal of the American Society of Training Directors*, 13, 3–9, 21–26; 14, 13–18, 28–32.

Kolb, D.A. (1984) *Experiential Learning*, Prentice-Hall, Englewood Cliffs, N.Y.

Latham, G.P. (1988) 'Human resource training and development', *Annual Review of Psychology*, 29, 545–582.

Latham, E.P. and L.M. Saari (1979) 'The application of Social Learning Theory to training supervisors through behavioural modelling', *Journal of Applied Psychology*, 64, 239–246.

Legge, K. (1984) *Evaluating Planned Organisational Change*, Academic Press, London.

Locke, E.A., K.N. Shaw, L.M. Saari and G.P. Latham (1981) 'Goal-setting and task performance 1969–80', *Psychological Bulletin*, 90, 1, 125–152.

McGarrell, E.R. (1984) 'An orientation system that builds productivity', *Personnel Administrator*, 29, 10, 75–85.

McGehee, W. and P.W. Thayer (1961) *Training in Business and Industry*, Wiley, New York.

McGregor, D. (1960) *The Human Side of Enterprise*, McGraw-Hill, New York.

Mager, R.F. (1962) *Preparing Objectives for Programmed Instruction*, Fearon, San Francisco.

Mager, R.F. and P. Pipe (1990) *Analysing Performance Problems*, 2nd ed. Kogan Page, London.

Massey, J.C. (1957) 'Postal carrier training,' *Journal of the American Society for Training and Development*, Sept/Oct.

Mayer, S.J. and J.S. Russell (1987) 'Behavior modeling training in organisations,' *Journal of Management*, 13, 21–40.

Mirvis, P.H. and B.A. Macy (1982) 'Evaluating program costs and benefits', ch. 17 in E.S. Seashore, E.E. Lawler, P.H. Mirvis and C. Camman, *Assessing Organisational Change*, Wiley, New York.

Parlett, M. and D. Hamilton (1977) 'Evaluation as a new approach to the study of innovative programmes', in D. Hamilton, D. Jenkins, C. King, B. MacDonald and M. Parlett (eds) *Beyond the Numbers Game*, Macmillan, London.

Patrick, J., I. Michael and A. Moore (1986) *Design for Learning*, Occupational Services Ltd, Aston Science Park, Birmingham.

Patton, M.C.E. (1978) *Utilization-focused Evaluation*, Sage, Beverly Hills.

Pearn, M. (1981) *CRAMP: A Guide to Training Decisions*, ITRU Research paper TRI, Industrial Training Research Unit, Cambridge.

Pedler, M. (ed.) (1983) *Action Learning in Practice*, Gower, Aldershot.

Pepper, A.D. (1984) *Managing the Training and Development Function*, Gower, Aldershot.

Pettigrew, A.M. (1975) 'Towards a political theory of organisational interventions', *Human Relations*, 28, 191–208.

Pettigrew, A.M., E.R. Jones and P.W. Reason (1982) *Training and Development Roles in their organisational setting*, Training Division, MSC, Sheffield.

Prophet, E. (1976) *Long-term Retention of Flying Skills: A Review of the Literature*, HUMRRO/FR-EDP-76-35 (Human Resources Research Organization) Alexandria, Virginia.

Rackham, N. and T. Morgan (1977) *Behavioural Analysis in Training*, McGraw-Hill, Maidenhead.

Randall, L.K. (1960) 'Evaluation: A training dilemma', *Journal of the American Society of Training Directors*, 14, 29–35.

Robson, M. (1982) *Quality Circles: A Practical Guide*, Gower, Aldershot.

Rossi, P.H., H.E. Freeman and S.R. Wright (1979) *Evaluation: A Systematic Approach*, Sage, Beverly Hills.

Rowland, V. (1970) *Evaluating and Improving Managerial Performance*, McGraw-Hill, New York.

Sashkin, M., W.C. Morris and L. Horst (1973) 'A comparison of social and organizational change models', *Psychological Review*, 50, 6.

Scriven, M. (1967) 'The Methodology of Evaluation', *AERA Monograph Series in Curriculum Evaluation*, 1, Rand McNally, Chicago.

Scriven, M. (1973) 'Goal-free evaluation', in E.R. House (ed.) *School Evaluation: The Politics and Process*, McCutchan, Berkeley, California.

Seashore, S.E., E.E. Lawler, P.H. Mirvis and C. Camman (1982) *Assessing Organisational Change*, Wiley, New York.

Skinner, B.F. (1954) 'The science of learning and the art of teaching,' in Lumsdaine, A.A. and R. Glaser (eds) *Teaching Machines and Programmed Learning*, NEA, Washington DC.

Stake, R.E. (ed.) (1975) *Evaluating the Arts in Education: A Responsive Approach*, Merrill, Columbus, Ohio.

Stammers, R. and J. Patrick (1975) *The Psychology of Training*, Methuen, London.

Stewart, A. and V. Stewart (1981) *Business Applications of Repertory Grids*, McGraw-Hill, Maidenhead.

Stone, D.L., H.G. Guertal and B. McIntosh (1984) 'The effects of feedback sequence and expertise of the rater on perceived feedback accuracy', *Personnel Psychology*, 37, 487–506.

Sykes, A.J.M. (1962) 'The effect of a supervisory training course on supervisors' perceptions and expectations of the role of management', *Human Relations*, 15, 227–244.

Tyler, R.W. (1950) *Basic Principles of Curriculum and Instruction Design*, University of Chicago Press, Chicago.

Vintor, K.L., A.O. Clark and J.W. Seybolt (1983) 'Assessment of training needs for supervisors,' *Personnel Administrator*, 28, 11, 49.

Warr, P., M. Bird and N. Rackham (1970) *Evaluation of Management Training*, Gower Press, London.

Weinstein, L.M. and E.S. Kasl (1982) 'How the training dollar is spent,' *Training and Development Journal*, Oct.

Weisbord, M. (1985) 'Team effectiveness theory', *Training and Development Journal*, Jan.

Wellens, J. (1979) 'Total training', *Industrial and Commercial Training*, Sept, 371–378.

Wetzel, S., P. Konoske and W. Montague (1983) *Estimating Skills Loss through a Navy Technical Pipeline*, NPRDC TR 84–7, Navy Personnel Research and Development Center, San Diego, California.

Wexley, K.N. (1984) 'Training in work organisations', *Annual Review of Psychology*, 31, 229–272.

Woodcock, M. (1979) *Team Development Manual*, Gower, Aldershot.

Woodman, R.W. and J.J. Sherwood (1980) 'The role of team development in organizational effectiveness: a critical review', *Psychological Bulletin*, 88, 1, 166–186.

Woodward, N. (1975) 'Cost benefit analysis of supervisor training', *Industrial Relations Journal*, 6, 2, 41–47.

Index

Further titles in the McGraw-Hill Training Series

THE BUSINESS OF TRAINING
Achieving Success in Changing World Markets
Trevor Bentley   ISBN 0-07-707328-2

DEVELOPING EFFECTIVE TRAINING SKILLS
Tony Pont   ISBN 0-07-707383-5

MAKING MANAGEMENT DEVELOPMENT WORK
Achieving Success in the Nineties
Charles Margerison   ISBN 0-07-707382-7

MANAGING PERSONAL LEARNING AND CHANGE
A Trainer's Guide
Neil Clark   ISBN 0-07-707344-4

HOW TO DESIGN EFFECTIVE TEXT-BASED OPEN
LEARNING:
A Modular Course
Nigel Harrison   ISBN 0-07-707355-X

HOW TO DESIGN EFFECTIVE COMPUTER BASED
TRAINING:
A Modular Course
Nigel Harrison   ISBN 0-07-707354-1

HOW TO SUCCEED IN EMPLOYEE DEVELOPMENT
Moving from Vision to Results
Ed Moorby   ISBN 0-07-707459-9

USING VIDEO IN TRAINING AND EDUCATION
Ashly Pinnington   ISBN 0-07-707384-3

TRANSFER OF LEARNING FOR TRAINERS
Julie Hay   ISBN 0-07-707470-X

79000